It Happened in France

It Happened in France

A Renowned Journalist's Account of Life Under the Occupation 1940–1944

Ernest Grimaud de Caux

Edited by François Eliet

Pen & Sword
MILITARY

First published in Great Britain in 2024 by
Pen & Sword Military
An imprint of Pen & Sword Books Limited
Yorkshire – Philadelphia

ISBN 978 1 39903 792 1

A CIP catalogue record for this book is available from the British Library

Typeset by Mac Style
Printed in the UK by CPI Group (UK) Ltd, Croydon, CR0 4YY.

MIX
Paper | Supporting responsible forestry
FSC® C013604
FSC www.fsc.org

Pen & Sword Books Limited incorporates the imprints of After the Battle, Atlas, Archaeology, Aviation, Discovery, Family History, Fiction, History, Maritime, Military, Military Classics, Politics, Select, Transport, True Crime, Air World, Frontline Publishing, Leo Cooper, Remember When, Seaforth Publishing, The Praetorian Press, Wharncliffe Local History, Wharncliffe Transport, Wharncliffe True Crime and White Owl.

For a complete list of Pen & Sword titles please contact

PEN & SWORD BOOKS LIMITED
47 Church Street, Barnsley, South Yorkshire, S70 2AS, England
E-mail: enquiries@pen-and-sword.co.uk
Website: www.pen-and-sword.co.uk
or
PEN AND SWORD BOOKS
1950 Lawrence Rd, Havertown, PA 19083, USA
E-mail: uspen-and-sword@casematepublishers.com
Website: www.penandswordbooks.com

Contents

Editor's Introduction

This book has been some time in the making. My granduncle first sought to have it published in the immediate after-war period, contacting his old colleagues at *The Times* for advice. However, as explained in a letter de Caux received through the Paris Correspondent of *The Times* in early 1945, the London publishing houses approached said that they couldn't consider such whilst printing paper was so short. They added that by the time supply improved it was likely that public interest in the Essays would have diminished, presumably on the basis that people wanted to move on with their lives and leave the war experience behind.

Many years later, de Caux's niece, Maureen Eliet (my mother), worked on the project and wrote a Personal Appreciation of her uncle, which is included in this book. When she died, my siblings were most thoughtful in insisting that the archive – including the original manuscript of the Essays as well as the Great War diaries, considerable professional and personal correspondence, and volumes of folders of *Times* articles – be kept together as one and were very kind in entrusting it to me.

I would characterise what I have done as a very mild editing of the Essays. They are the same length as the originals and the essence of the narrative and views expressed are faithful to what de Caux wrote. There was never any question of it being otherwise. However, on the basis of certain constructions and vocabulary being somewhat cumbersome and perhaps belonging to a different age, I have changed these slightly to allow an easier flow of his prose. In this connection, it is interesting that his *Printing House Square* obituary says that "If memory serves – it seems not incredible – there was a hint that long residence abroad was beginning to inject some un-English phrases into his writing." This in no way diminishes the learning, thoughtfulness, and breath of experience that underlie what he wrote.

Apart from my siblings, I would like to thank the Publisher, Pen and Sword Books, and their Publishing Manager, Brigadier Henry Wilson, for taking on this project, as well as Matthew Jones, Production Manager, and the rest of the team, for seeing it through. David Walsh, former Second Master of Tonbridge School and author of three books on public schools and the two World Wars, provided invaluable help and encouragement throughout, also writing the Great War segment of the biography. *The Times* Archivist and Deputy Archivist, Nick Mays and Anne Jensen, received me very kindly in their magnificent new facility and found me the relevant files, all in pristine condition. My neighbour, Phil Stavrinou, kindly produced the maps. I am grateful to my former long-time secretary, Gillian Rimmer, for her re-typing of the entire text. Lastly, I owe a debt to my wife, Jane, whose commitment and enthusiasm for the work provided the bedrock support to see it through.

De Caux whereabouts Great War 1914-18

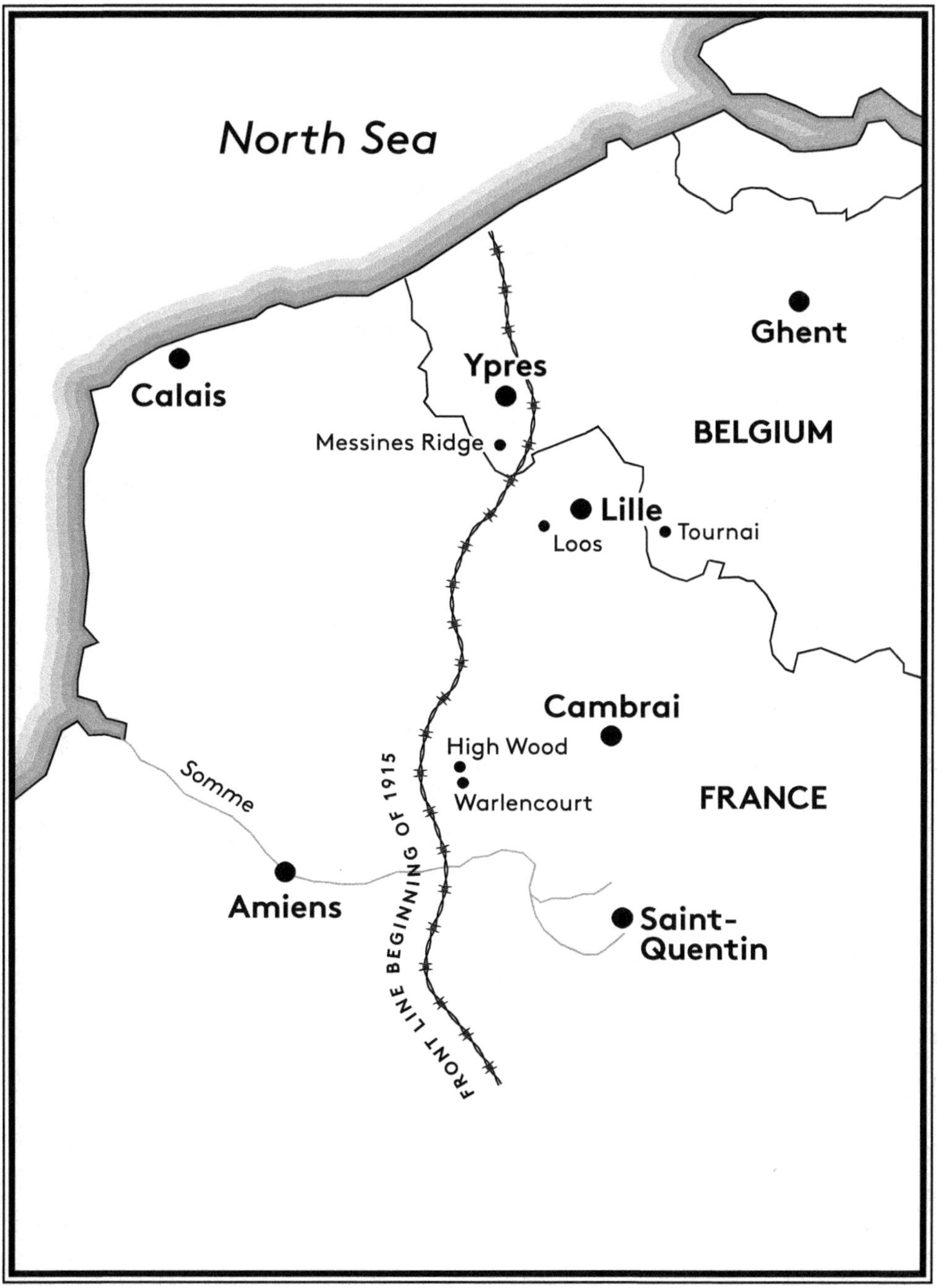

September 1915 - Loos
September 1916 - High Wood (Somme)
October 1916 - Warlencourt (Somme)
June 1917 - Messines Ridge (prelude to third battle of Ypres)
November 1918 - Tournai

De Caux whereabouts during Civil War

July 1936 - February 1937 - Madrid
September - October 1937 - Valencia
November - December 1937 - Barcelona
1938 - Hendaye
January - February 1939 - Perpignan

De Caux whereabouts during German occupation 1940-44

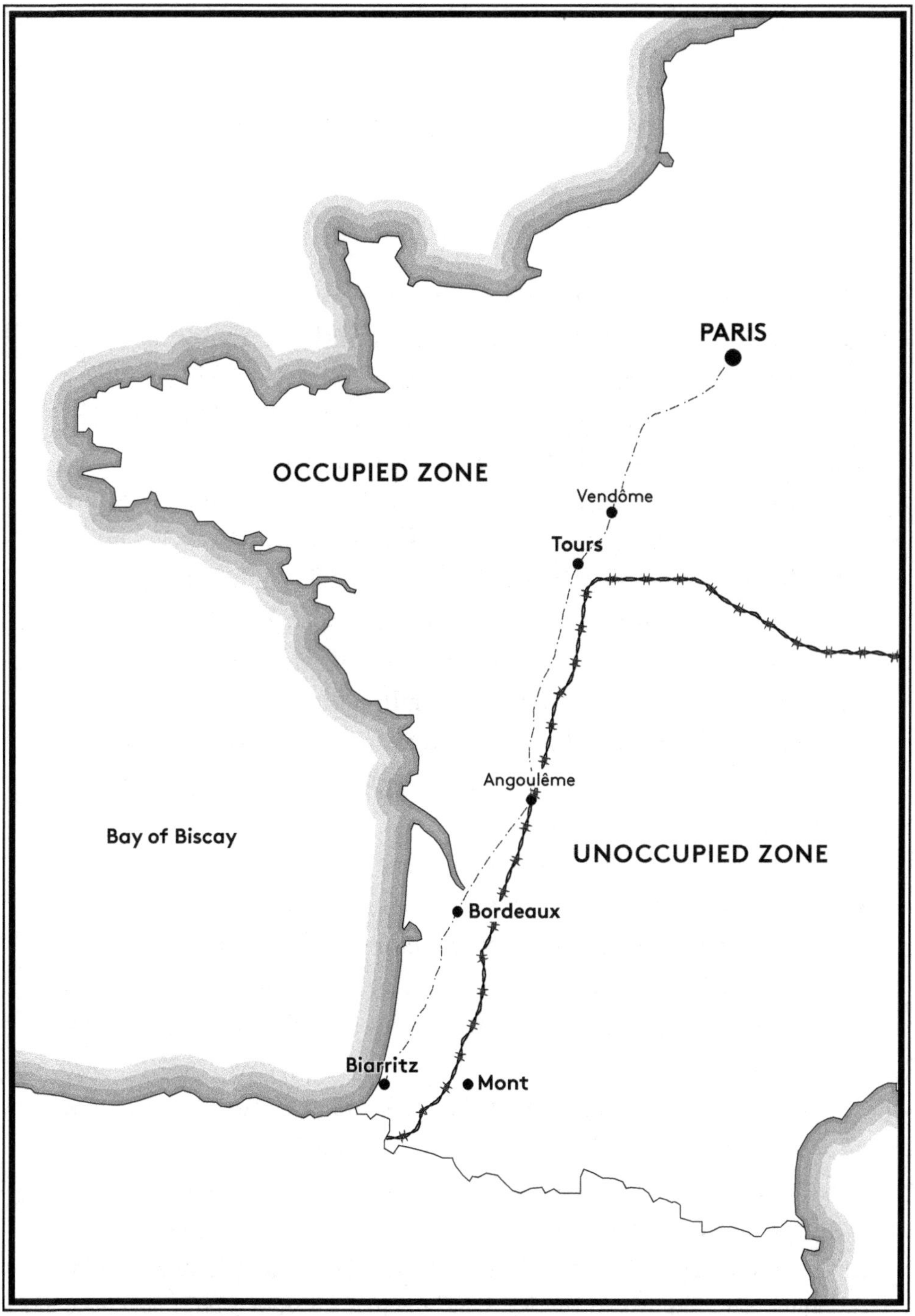

Journey Paris - Biarritz c. June 10th-18th 1940

Demarcation line June 1940 - November 1942

De Caux was banished from the coast to Mont in early 1943 after his release from prison

Biography of Ernest Grimaud de Caux

It was de Caux's lot in life that he was born at a time that would destine him to experience four years' frontline duty in the Great War; observe, report on and live through the Spanish Civil War from a primary vantage point; and be subjected to the entire period of German Occupation of France in the Second World War.

De Caux was born in Lucan, on the outskirts of Dublin, on 28 July 1879. His maternal grandfather, Sir James W. Mackey, was twice Lord Mayor of Dublin, in 1866 and 1873. The family business, a seed wholesaling and retailing company established in 1777, carried on in Dublin until 2007 under the name of Mackeys. Though he never actually lived in Ireland as an adult, he retained a deep love of the country. He remained for many years a Director of the business, and as with everything with which he was connected, he always kept a keen interest in its fortunes.

His mother, Mary Mackey, was Irish, but his father was a Frenchman serving in his country's foreign service where he held the position of Counsellor in various American cities before being posted to Dublin in 1875 and finally to Jersey in 1888 where he retired as Consul General in 1900. The family then moved to Rennes in 1901 and subsequently to Biarritz.

After his schooling in Jersey, de Caux continued his further education at Senlis College, the Sorbonne and the University of Rennes.

Attracted at an early age to Spanish culture and language (a third language he was to speak fluently) he moved to Spain in 1904, working first as secretary to Count Albiz, a lawyer with a large international practice, subsequently in the British Consulate, and in 1910 beginning his 30-year association with *The Times*. However, there was to be a long break in this association for the duration of the Great War.

The outbreak of war on 4 August 1914 opened up a new chapter in de Caux's life and he enlisted initially in the French Army. His first regiment was the 23rd Territorial Infantry as 'Soldat de Premier Classe', but his bilingual skills were in demand as the Allied armies expanded and he transferred to the 'Corps of Interpreters'. It was in this role as interpreter and liaison officer that he was assigned to the Post Office Rifles (8th London Regiment) when they landed in France at Le Havre in March 1915 as part of 140 Infantry Brigade in the 47th (London) Division. The Post Office Rifles (POR) was a London battalion of the Territorial Force, about 900 strong, and consisting mainly of employees of the Post Office. As such it had a support system and intimacy about it which was to stand it in good stead through the years of fighting in France.

De Caux was with the POR from its first day in France until it was disbanded in February 1918. His role as interpreter and liaison officer to the POR had widened in 1916 to perform the same role for 140 Inf Bde, consisting of three or four infantry battalions and other supporting arms.

He kept a meticulous and detailed diary from March 1915 to beyond the end of the war, and this very personal account, handwritten in ten books, formed the basis of an account of the battalion's war which he lodged in the Imperial War Museum. His primary role was to ensure good relations between the British battalion and brigade and the French army and civil authorities. Much of his time appears to have been spent in finding billets for the units, which moved around very regularly behind the trench lines, ensuring that food and shelter were available and smoothing over any disputes between the soldiers and the homeowners in whose houses and fields they were billeted. He also liaised with the French military authorities, helped the battalion's transport officer and quartermaster who were responsible for logistical support, visited the wounded in hospital and assisted the padre with church services in the field and burials of dead soldiers.

Although he did not take part in front-line military operations, his diaries often refer to him being under shellfire and bombardment, and record many visits in or close to the front line. He wore the uniform of the French army and was effectively treated as an officer, eating his meals in the officers' mess and spending time with individual battalion officers, with whom he clearly had very cordial relations. One of the privileges of his position was to have his own horse, which was kept at the transport lines and was his main means of scouting new billets. In a letter to his mother in March 1915, just after he had joined the POR, he describes his pride in riding down to the station just behind the Colonel. By the time of the battalion's disbandment in February 1918, only de Caux and two other officers of the original cadre of March 1915 were still part of it.

Territorial battalions had less pre-war training than those of the professional army but they were in better shape to undertake front-line duties than the volunteers who flooded into Kitchener's New Army in 1914. As a consequence, the POR were never far from the heat of battle and took part in major offensives at Loos in September 1915, the Somme in the autumn of 1916 and the capture of Messines Ridge in June 1917, the prelude to the Third Battle of Ypres. They also suffered a regular stream of casualties in the attritional trench warfare which went on between these major battles. Apart from occasional periods of leave back home, de Caux was present throughout all this, observing and carefully recording the life of the battalion and brigade and his part in it.

A few excerpts from his diary give a flavour of the war and reveal the part he played. He was a sharp observer of battlefield tactics, as this first excerpt shows. It follows early trench fighting in which the POR was involved around Festubert and Givenchy from April-June 1915:

> *June 18 (At Noeux-les-Mines and Vermelles) More rumours of attack and reserves moved up again. Sharp fusillade during night for few moments on working party. During day some heavy stuff comes over and sharp burst of shrapnel on level crossing at 8pm just misses Deverell riding up from Noeux.... I have been three months with PORs and have seen something of the British army and its methods of fighting.*

The material, both human and other, is magnificent, but the staff work inefficient and the strategy bad. In none of the attacks at Festubert and Givenchy has the cohesion between the artillery and infantry been adequate. Infantry has been left without artillery support and worse still without infantry support. Attacks have been launched without wire being cut and without definitive objective... One after another the British attacks round La Bassée have failed with very heavy loss. Trenches are taken time and again but the men get bombed out the same or next day. Night attacks are now à la mode but don't meet with better success. Tremendous grousing is heard in every mess against the staff ......their system of moving regiments constantly from place to place has great disadvantages. A Bn that remains sometime in the same section of trench gets to know it better and takes more interest in it than a series of different regiments. Moving in and out causes much more wear and tear on the troops themselves not to speak of the unhappy inhabitants of Noeux-les-Mines. The old lady who took in HQ had been woken up three nights running with different regiments. Also, since so much transport is noticeable, villages are much oftener shelled than before when the same Fr regiment remained for six months at a time in the same billets.

The first major offensive involving the POR was at Loos in September and October 1915, a costly and unsuccessful battle:

Oct 13 I ride to Haillicourt at 9am with Clarke to see owner of field where our transport stopped and who claims damages (60fr). Beautiful morning as mild as Spring. As we return from ridge this side of Noeux we see active shelling going on all along front from Hulluch to Cambrin. At 1pm precisely dense clouds of smoke go up and the wind seems favourable. The operation as ordered is for the 1st Div to seize the German trenches over the Hulluch road on a length of about 1500 yds and dig in on a favourable position in front of Hulluch, send a patrol into that village and occupy it if possible. Our Div is in support for assault to be delivered on Hohenzollern Redoubt and Fosse 8 ... I saw some shelling over Fosse 8 and what seemed to be a gas attack on Hulluch at 4.15pm. Wounded going through say that things going well but that they found Huns in front trench when they got there. After dinner visited clearing hospital. Several of the wounded were suffering from gas. All said it was a hard fight and a Jock told the same old story of wire uncut and good Hun bombing. Another Jock with a bullet in his chest was complacently smoking a cigarette.

In September 1916, the POR joined the British offensive on the Somme and took part in two significant attacks – on High Wood on 15 September and the Butte de Warlencourt on 7 October. In these two actions, eleven POR officers were killed and eleven wounded, a dreadful toll when one considers that the battalion roll would normally only include about twenty officers. Over 700 other ranks were killed or wounded. De Caux's diary records the attack on High Wood and its aftermath:

Sept 15 Zero was fixed for 6.20 and the intense fire about then woke me up. Deverell (POR transport officer) *about 10am tells us Bde was held up in wood but that Divs on our wings are doing well….All our reserve of officers called up this morning. Our casualties 150 men and 5 officers. About 1,000 prisoners went through here today in batches of 125 – those I saw were fine men, haggard looking……*

When the Somme offensive petered out in November 1916, the POR moved to the Ypres Salient for the next ten months. This was a long period of trench warfare in the most dangerous sector of the British front. The battalion moved in and out of the front line and de Caux was always busy on his liaison duty and in finding and preparing new billets. The POR took part in the capture of Messines Ridge between 3 and 12 June 1917 and was then withdrawn and sent to the front near Arras in September, becoming involved two months later in the Cambrai battle.

In his diary entry for 21 October, de Caux recorded the fact that he had been awarded the Military Medal, which was a decoration awarded to other ranks for 'acts of gallantry and devotion to duty under fire'.

> *Oct 21 Sunday. Walk down to Mass at Div cinema 9am and on to Trafalgar Camp to go billeting with Peel at Maroeuil. Alexander congratulates me on my Military Medal. First news! At dinner time Kennedy* (Brigadier-General commanding 140 Bde) *congratulates me officially. Crisp and bright sun.*

In February 1918 the 1/8th London (Post Office Rifles) was disbanded. By the beginning of 1918 manpower shortages were making themselves felt and the battalion's history records: 'Military requirements prompted the dispersal of this unit, partly owing to the difficulty of their being reinforced and partly the need for other units to be reinforced. For those officers and other ranks who had made the 1/8th their military home for so long and had fought together so often and so successfully, it was a hard blow to find that they were to be scattered in many directions'. De Caux himself remained with 140 Brigade, serving the billeting and liaison needs of the four battalions within it.

In his diary he recorded the end of the war:

> *Nov 11 Dull morning. Rode off with Dev at 8.30 for La Tombe. On the way meet Pontius Pilate who stops his car to tell us the armistice will be on from 11am onwards. We look at our watches and note the 1hr and 17 mins to go. As we ride down towards Tournai Dev shouts the news to everyone, soldiers, refugees and civilians. The latter mostly reply civilly 'Merci monsieur' as if we were the dispensers of the long-awaited blessing. Far behind us the cannon is still rumbling.*

There is no doubting the great esteem in which de Caux was held by the officers of both the POR and 140 Brigade. When he married, he was presented with a handsome silver salver inscribed with the names of surviving officers with whom he had served and the inscription:

'France 1915–19. To Ernest Grimaud de Caux. On the occasion of his marriage and as a mark of the very high esteem in which he was held by all ranks of the Post Office Rifles and 140 Infantry Brigade Headquarters'.

When de Caux died in 1960, an anonymous officer of the POR wrote this generous tribute: 'I am sure that all those who served in the First Battalion of the Post Office Rifles (8th London Regiment) will have learned with great regret of the death of de Caux, our interpreter and good and valued friend. We went to France in March 1915 and de Caux joined us there. We found ourselves in what was to us a strange land of mining villages, farms and occasionally a small country town, and it was his job to make life smooth for us in our new surroundings. Unlike some interpreters, he had an admirable command of English – in fact, so good was his English that the wits of the mess professed to doubt if he really spoke French. But above all he had a most delightful personality and unassuming manner. I can remember, as a harassed company commander, going with him to find billets in towns where the inhabitants did not relish the prospect but allowed de Caux's quiet and courteous approach to persuade them. I think we were a well-behaved battalion but there were times when for instance 'spy mania' led to the killing of pigeons in a French family's loft; or a parade was held on the one and only grass field of a village and it took all de Caux's tact to get us out of trouble .... It goes without saying that de Caux was a brave man. I never remember seeing him ruffled by any circumstances, however unpleasant they might be. As time went on, and casualties became heavier, de Caux's experience was a great factor in keeping up our morale. We could always rely on him – he was one of us.'

With the end of the war it was time to return to civilian life. His position with *The Times* in Madrid had not been held for him for the duration of the war and he was concerned as to whether he would be able to return to it. He was thus much relieved by a meeting he had in February 1919 with Henry Wickham Steed, then Editor of *The Times,* and on which de Caux reported in a letter to his mother, "I saw Wickham Steed today and he was very kind indeed. He said he was delighted to see I had come through the war and that *The Times* would be very glad to see me back in Madrid" (letter 26 February 1919 Private archive).

Thus, he returned to Spain and his old job as correspondent, reporting over the subsequent twenty years on the turbulent events of the inter-war period, dictatorship of Primo de Rivera, fall of the monarchy, establishment of the republic, and subsequent Civil War.

De Rivera's period in office was dominated by the war in Morocco but de Caux was also concerned about the constitutional legitimacy of the *régime.* In a letter to Ralph Deakin (Imperial and Foreign News Editor) he wrote: "More will be heard of the constitutional problem in Spain. Every month that passes widens the breach between King Alfonso and his subjects. The King's position may be outlined briefly as follows: His Sovereignty is not absolute. The Nation shares it and the duties of Nation and Monarch towards each other are regulated by this co-sovereignty. It is His Majesty's duty and obligation to convoke a new Cortes within three months of the dissolution of the last elected Cortes, whatever the cause of dissolution may be. To avoid implicating the King in the breach of law caused by the *coup d'état* of September 13,1923, Primo's early manifestos carefully stated that normality would be restored within 90 days. But later, pretence was thrown to the winds. The three months expired and when, shortly thereafter, the Speakers of the Senate and of the Chamber of Deputies proceeded to the Palace and reminded the King of his obligation, they were sent away empty-handed. For three years now, with the tacit consent, if not the open approval of the King, the Marquis de Estella (de Rivera) has continued to deride parliamentary institutions …" (letter 26 August 1926 *The Times* de Caux archive).

Here was an early example of the undermining of constitutional procedure which, with other factors, would lead to the upheavals of the 1930s and, ultimately, the Civil War.

De Caux did nonetheless have regard for de Rivera. At the end of the Military Directory in January 1930, he wrote of him that, to his task, he had brought "great energy, resourcefulness and geniality". However, he added "opposition to his rule grew" and "The Army – the instrument which brought him to power – came at last to distrust the usefulness of his continued rule." (*The Times* 29 January 1930).

In these times, newspapers held a prime position in the dissemination of news and his articles were read, and treated with importance, by those in authority. A case in point is a letter to de Caux from Deakin where he mentions a meeting he (Deakin) had had with King Alfonso. "Just a line to let you know that I had a talk with Don Alfonso here (in London) the day before he left for Madrid. He was perfectly friendly but suggested that our Madrid Correspondent needed looking after sometimes … His complaint against you was chiefly that you saw the shady and more insidious side of events and gave rather more prominence than he would have liked to the enemies of the Throne… The only reason I mention it is because I got the impression that he would welcome a talk with you. I don't know how you feel about it" (letter 24 March 1931 *The Times* de Caux archive).

In his reply de Caux says "As regards soliciting an audience, I do not see any use in it at all. It would only increase Don Alfonso's resentment if, after having publicly solicited an audience and being received, I should have to write reports such as those published that have incurred the royal displeasure … I cannot command events nor refrain from reporting them. That is the rub." (letter 29 March 1931 *The Times* de Caux archive).

Major events followed shortly thereafter. On 14 April 1931, following the general election which gave the forces of the Left a majority, King Alfonso was obliged to leave Madrid, and the following day de Caux filed an article detailing the tumultuous events – how they'd been precipitated during the day from an earlier point, when nothing was expected, to the King departing the Palace that same evening; the Republican crowds gathering in the streets without hindrance from the forces of order; newly elected Republican representatives taking office in the regional cities without the normal delay for validation; the outgoing Prime Minister, declaring in the late afternoon that there was no crisis, to the incoming President announcing a few hours later that "the Republic was triumphant and in peaceful possession of office", appealing for "that respect for order which had made the revolution a model one". De Caux knew that the completeness of the report, covering every important aspect of the day's developments, was key to the reader's obtaining a full appreciation of the situation.

In the same report, and perhaps revealing something of himself, he added that "the breathless rapidity with which a Monarchy fifteen centuries old has been swept away with no opposition from such hitherto steadfast forces as the Army and the Church, which has in the past inspired its faithful on many a previous occasion to fly to arms for the Monarchy, is nothing short of amazing, and leaves observers in Madrid dumbfounded." (*The Times* 15 April 1931)

De Caux was in Madrid at the time of the Uprising in July 1936 as well as for the subsequent eight months, during which the Nationalists advanced through the great cities of the South and West, taking also a broad swathe of northern central territory extending from Galicia to Navarre, relieving the siege of the Alcázar in Toledo, before attempting, in October and November, an assault on the capital itself, which was to be saved for the Republic by the arrival of large reinforcements of International Brigades.

His first uncensored report of the Civil War appeared in *The Times* of 2 August, two weeks after the start of the Uprising. He described the situation as "A clash of extremes", involving "Strife without quarter".

The first paragraph of the report deserves to be quoted. "A fortnight has passed since the first flash of revolt started a conflict that is shaking the Republic to its foundations. All is turmoil and strife; the outlook a cloud through which two alternatives loom like cliffs. Should the revolt triumph – and viewed from Madrid it cannot win without foreign intervention – a Fascist regime would be the result, against which rebellion would continue until drowned in blood. Should the sedition be suppressed (and that will certainly be a long business) the Liberal Republic of 1931 must perish in the process. Two extremes are at each other's throats. One must succumb. There is no central force strong enough to separate them. The story of the Rising so far bears out that conviction." A paragraph written only two weeks into a three-year Civil War but containing much that was prophetic.

This report, typical of many filed over subsequent months, described the general lawlessness in the city as well as the persecution of the Religious Orders – "Firing never ceased all over the town. Groups on foot or in cars taken out of public and private garages 'for the service of the Republic' fired at every flapping shutter or sign of movement at upper windows or on rooftops. Wild boys chasing about in all kinds of vehicles fired madly. Many churches and convents were looted or burnt … Warriors were having a glorious time, with pistols and guns, plenty of ammunition, and no need to account for its use … Nuns and priests were fleeing for their lives; many of the latter lost them."

De Caux managed to send twenty-two such reports, in uncensored form, over the period August 1936 to February 1937. Had they been sent through the censor's hands, they would have borne no comparison, in truth or completeness, to what he actually sent. To do so he sometimes needed to resort to ingenious methods. One such is recounted by an American (Stanford) academic, Ronald Hilton, who found himself in Madrid in the early-mid 1930s and who knew de Caux.

"… foreigners like me who were not engaged in essential work were ordered to leave Spain … I called on my friend and mentor, *Times* correspondent Ernest Grimaud de Caux, for whom I had a deep affection. I asked him if there was anything I could do. He said I could take with me a report he had written on the situation in Madrid, which the censor would not have passed. Knowing that this would be dangerous, I replied that it would certainly be confiscated. He told me not to worry and to return in the afternoon. When I returned, he gave me a book, *Strange Adventures at Sea*, and said that it was the report to be delivered to *The Times*. When I looked puzzled, saying I could not find it, he expressed satisfaction that his trick had worked. He had typed his report on rice paper and folded it so that it would fit into the spine of the book. I clutched the book and bade de Caux farewell.

"… my train finally reached Valencia station, where we were taken by bus to the port. There were sand-bagged barricades all the way and the buses weaved their way through them. When we got to the port everyone was carefully searched. Some were stripped completely. Fortunately, little attention was paid to me and I walked to a waiting launch clutching in my hand the precious book de Caux had entrusted to me.

"Warships from various nations were standing off the port and we were taken to HMS *Devonshire* …Next day the ship arrived in Marseilles, where I mailed the sacred document to *The Times,* mission accomplished. The report appeared under the headline 'The Tragedy of Spain. First Uncensored News from Madrid.' It attracted great attention." (Hilton, Ronald (2000). *Spain, 1931–36, From Monarchy to Civil War: An Eye Witness Account)*

Whilst he reported events as he saw them, there were nonetheless dangers inherent to de Caux's work. Since everything he was witnessing was happening in government-controlled territory, what he wrote was hardly flattering to the Republic. His colleagues at *The Times* were concerned and Deakin wrote to him "We have noted your desire to remain in the Capital and wish only that you should bear in mind that your personal safety should be put first" (letter 4 January 1937 de Caux *Times* archive). Indeed, a telephone message of 16 February 1937 from Deakin asks "Can you please come out? The Editor begs you to. We should very much like to see you here and think you ought to come." De Caux replied the following day – "Please thank the Editor for his kind message. I will bear it in mind when the time comes."

However, as the war continued, the danger increased. There was no mean risk involved in filing these uncensored reports in the face of threats. The Marxist paper *Politika*, which sent many people to their death, denounced de Caux by name and had him called before the Special Investigation Bureau of the Defence Junta. Deakin reports what de Caux then told him. "After two separate interrogatories I was able to persuade them that *The Times* published news from many different sources. So I got off with the warning … about their dislike of uncensored articles … It is proclaimed that the S.C. and O.O.C.

(Special Correspondent and Our Own Correspondent) are one and the same person in Madrid. This has placed me in an impossible position and I can no longer venture to send you Special Articles" (Internal Memorandum 18 March 1937 de Caux *Times* Archive).

He travelled a lot throughout the two subsequent years, firstly to Valencia and then spending considerable time in Barcelona, effectively following the Republican Government as it moved in response to the Nationalist advance. There were also periodic visits back to Madrid, breaks home in Biarritz, and one visit to London. As the war progressed and eventually faced its inexorable end he reported from Perpignan on the retreat of Republican forces across the Pyrenees and the issues they faced as refugees.

Throughout this period Deakin undoubtedly treated de Caux as the Senior Correspondent in Spain. In keeping with this, in June 1937, Deakin advised de Caux that *The Times* would be sending the young H.A.R. (Kim) Philby to Francoist Spain to cover the Nationalist side. Deakin asked Philby to meet with de Caux in Biarritz on his way out to Salamanca. De Caux subsequently reported back "I have met Philby. Holburn (Berlin Correspondent who had been in Nationalist Spain for a period) brought him to lunch … and we had a long talk afterwards. You have got an exceptionally promising young fellow in P." (Letter 15 June 1937 de Caux *Times* archive).

In a retrospective piece, produced as two articles by *The Times* (11 and 15 February 1939), he wrote that "During the last quarter of a century, monarchy, dictatorship, and republic have in turn failed to reconcile the factions. Failure of government is the root cause of the war. The constitutional monarch did not show himself constitutional, the dictator was unable to give a long enough period of service, and the Republic failed through weakness." It would be in Spain's interest to remain neutral in any coming international conflict and he could not see how Germany or Italy could constrain the Spanish government to enter any such war on their side. He thought there would be a gradual return to normal relations with Britain and France.

Thus, at the end of the Civil War, and because of the way the war had evolved, he found himself in southwest France, where, as previously mentioned, he had a family home. The question then became 'could he return to Spain, to his work, and to his flat in Madrid?' Geoffrey Dawson, then Editor of The Times, wrote to de Caux on the matter: "It seems to me that in his own interests Franco would be very wise to welcome you in Madrid forthwith. I shall look forward with great interest to seeing what happens in this connection. They tell me – I do not know with what truth – that there are two schools of thought on the subject among his advisers. Meanwhile however I am all for your going home to Biarritz and keeping a general eye on Spain from that point of vantage." (letter 28 February 1939 Private archive)

The outcome was that the new régime took the view that his Spanish resident's permit should be revoked.

The Duke of Alba – Nationalist Ambassador to London during the Civil War – told de Caux that this was because he had not come over to report from the Nationalist side when he had had the opportunity of doing so. This is not altogether convincing since his reports of the lawlessness he saw in Madrid were in fact helpful to the Nationalists. It is true, however, from Deakin's report of a visit to *The Times'* offices by Luis Bolín, Franco's Press Director, in June 1937, that de Caux was indeed invited but he was sceptical of what he might learn on a 'conducted' tour and also wary that any such visit to the Nationalist side would undermine his subsequent position with the Republican government.

De Caux's own words on this matter probably offer the true reason for the revocation of the visa. "…I do not think that Franco will allow me to return forthwith to Madrid when he re-installs government in the Capital. In his desire to cut with the past I shall probably be included, for he or rather his police will not favour a correspondent with so many contacts. They will naturally prefer a greener bird and Philby is already *persona grata*." (Letter 23 February 1939 de Caux *Times* archive)

Unable to return to Madrid and still employed by *The Times*, de Caux was posted to the Paris office in December 1939 which was where he found himself when the Germans attacked through the Ardennes on 10 May 1940. The Essays in this book pick up his account of the subsequent four years from this point, the desperate first two months encompassing the Fall of France, chaos of refugees fleeing, fall of the Reynaud government and appointment of Pétain as *Président du Conseil* (16 June), signing of the Armistice (22 June), completion of the Occupation down the entire Atlantic Coast to Hendaye (last days of June), destruction by the British of the French Fleet in North Africa (3 July), and legal establishment of the Vichy regime (10 July).

On the evening of 9 June, the Minister of Propaganda of the French Government held a conference with the representatives of the foreign press, which de Caux attended. They were assured that the government had no intention of leaving Paris, but on the following day this is precisely what it did, travelling first to Tours and then to Bordeaux. De Caux, along with other foreign correspondents, followed. He was French and, having unsuccessfully attempted, amidst the confusion and chaos of the time, to communicate with *The Times* through the British Consulate in Bordeaux, after non-French nationals had left the country, he decided to move on to Biarritz.

It is difficult to imagine the sheer scale of the political event and the circumstances surrounding the life-changing decision he was obliged to take in Bordeaux – go on down to Biarritz or leave for England. The Germans weren't far; he was unable to do his work and, from the moment he would leave Bordeaux to drive South, he knew he would be leaving a job he loved; colleagues in the Press were encouraging him to go to England; and his wife, who was with him, was English. Against this, in leaving, he would have felt he was abandoning his country and also his only living sister who lived alone with her housekeeper at the family home in Biarritz. There was also the reality, to which he would have been very sensitive, that he was effectively proxy father to his ten year old niece (also in Biarritz), daughter of his beloved deceased sister Emilie, and to whom he felt a special responsibility.

It was at this point that, at his own instigation and as he had realised was inevitable, his long association with *The Times* came to an end.

In his letter from Bordeaux to Deakin of 19 June he wrote "I am preparing to fade away to my home at Biarritz. There are several reasons for this, one being that if I do not go now while the going is good I may get stuck here, which would be a pity when I am so near home. Also because as the Ministry of Information has been suppressed, the Police are taking over the supervision of the Press and have asked me to register as *The Times* representative, supply two photographs, etc. This I do not want to do in case, as seems very likely, a Gestapo agent will shortly be examining the French Police records." He covers various other points in the letter and then signs off "I would like to thank you very sincerely for many kindnesses received. Farewell and long live England." (de Caux *Times* archive)

He was in Biarritz throughout the Occupation except for a fifteen-month period, from April 1943, when, after interrogation and a three-week imprisonment by the Gestapo, he was exiled away from the coast and lived, in very difficult circumstances, in the countryside outside Pau. The Occupation of the southwest of France came to an end in August 1944, two months after D-Day, when the Germans realised the game was up and began their retreat.

The matter of de Caux's return to Spain had been off the table since the Franco-Spanish border had effectively been closed for the duration of the war. Transport and communications remained difficult for a considerable period after the end of the war but by this point six years had passed since the end of the Civil War and Spain needed to re-integrate itself into a world of normal international relations. It was in this context that he wrote to a colleague at *The Times* in May 1945 that despite "the strained relations between Paris and Madrid … and besides the possibility of the ancient 1939 veto being raised again … I have hopes that before the end of June my wife and I will be across the Bidassoa" (letter of 28 May 1945 Private archive). These hopes were in fact realised, as evidenced by a card to Deakin from Madrid, dated July 1945.

It has been written in various quarters that he was a supporter of the Nationalist cause, holding generally conservative and monarchical views, and that he was 'tolerated' by the Republicans, given his unfavourable reports. He was, of course, a product of his times – cataclysm of the Great War and political turbulence of the 30s – and of his family background – Diplomatic Corps and business. With this, and his devout faith, he would have been a natural supporter of the established system and horrified by the breakdown of civil order. But there is also the reality of Franco's lengthy veto of his return to Spain, hardly a sign of political proximity. The truth may have been simpler – de Caux was reporting on what he observed, and given that he was based in the Republican sector and given the horrors of the Civil War, this was bound to cast a poor light on whichever party was responsible, as it happened in this case, the Republican side.

He lived out his retirement in Madrid, enjoying his wide circle of friends and continuing to follow Spanish affairs, maintaining his prolific correspondence, and making frequent visits to Biarritz, London and Dublin. He also used this period to support family members in various ways with his kindly engaged and caring involvement and advice.

In 1921 he married Olive Holmes whom he had met in Madrid. She was a strong personality who helped him in his career. In the Printing House Square obituary (*The Times* in-house publication) of de Caux it says that "sometimes Mrs. de Caux – an equally sympathetic character – dictated the messages (report copy). She had a rich, Spanish-sounding voice that made us think of Carmen in the opera, or of a tall lady in a black mantilla, an impression not entirely dispelled when she came to see us in London." There is also no doubt that she played a major role in getting him out of prison, haranguing the upper echelons of German authority at the Kommandantur until they'd had enough. She died in London in 1959.

De Caux himself died at his home in Madrid on 28 March 1960. He is buried in the British Cemetery there.

A Personal Appreciation

I came by the manuscript of this book – or rather typewritten mémoire – when I was clearing out the house of my aunt, Alice de Caux, the author's sister, in 1969. Having myself lived during the war years in Biarritz, I was intrigued, and put it aside carefully in the knowledge that its contents were interesting both as personal memories and historically.

I shall try, in writing this appreciation of my uncle Ernest de Caux ("Nesto" for me), in part a European before his time, belonging as he did to Ireland, France and Spain, to depict the character of a man who meant much to me in my childhood and youth.

These Essays were all written between 1940 and 1944. They are partly autobiographical and partly reflections about French politics and French leaders at the time of the Fall of France and during the war years. His considerable experience as a journalist for nearly thirty years qualified him for this task.

He was a man who lived through major early twentieth century events and was able to give an account of them. But to me, he was much more. He communicated to me his great love of nature. It may have been picking blackberries along the lanes of the Basque countryside when I was a child, or years later walking by the upper lake of Glendalough in the Wicklow mountains (he was then nearing eighty). I believe he introduced skiing to Spain, and his granite 'chalet' in the Guadarrama, below the Navacerrada Pass, was the first to be built in that region.

I remember particularly the time after he and his wife had been deported from the Coastal Zone in 1943 and they were living in a cottage lent to them by the local landlord. It had no running water, but he made little of it. What he was proud of was his 'potager', his vegetable patch, and to this day I remember the flavour of the little cherry tomatoes he grew, warmed by the sun and just off the vine.

Many traits of his personality spring to mind, one of them being his marvellous gift as a guide. I travelled with him through Spain in 1949, and how he communicated to me his love for that country and his memories, remains sharp, be it eating a roasted suckling pig in Toledo, or looking down in Granada on the Albaicín, the gypsy quarter, with its lights, its music and its mysteries. He was thrifty too. His mémoire was typed on the back of old invoices and letters going back to his father's or even his grandfather's time. He never wasted anything and I remember when he came to visit us sometimes in Dublin, he would rush out when he heard the milk delivery cart and gather the droppings of the horse for our garden!

But most of all he was kind. When in Spain, he employed "Paca" who was his cook for many years, firstly as a young girl. Then she married a *guardia civil,* had a young son, and was widowed. He took her on with the boy, *Ramón*, and saw to the education of this young man. It was no mean feat lodging him in their not very spacious flat in Zurbarán and on his modest income. And when it came to the sad and long-lasting illness of his wife Olive (she had Alzheimer's), I quote from a letter he sent me dated 10 January 1957: "I have never envied money but now I wish I had enough to organise a home for us with the necessary personnel. Separation is terribly hard, for me as for her. When together, in the numerous lucid moments, we can console each other. There are still some sweet times. But when we are apart, life is desolate and bleak indeed." And that is when he had to take the decision to bring Olive to England to be cared for in a home run by the National Health Service (she had English nationality). And he came to live there at a friend's house so that he could visit her every day.

I have his last letter to me, written six days before his death, in a rather wobbly hand. Practically his last sentence to me is: "I would like to give the kids a decent bicycle for Easter. Would you buy a good one and let me know the damage." Then, "The weather is getting nice and one can sniff summer in the air."

Finally, I would like to mention an extract from a letter to *The Times* that C. Oldfield, a good friend of my uncle, wrote after his death. "He was a truly noble man and it would never have occurred to him that he would remain, and always will remain, such an example and an inspiration."

Maureen McGuire Eliet
2000

Niece of de Caux, Maureen McGuire Eliet was born in Dublin in 1930 and died there in 2013. She spent her childhood and youth in Biarritz before marrying and moving to Ireland with her husband in 1953. She retained a strong connection to Biarritz throughout her life, maintaining a home there until her death.

Preface

IT HAPPENED IN FRANCE is something of a pot-pourri – in part extracts from a personal record kept from week to week, in part collection of essays or rather articles written on the spur of the moment almost through force of habit.

The only excuse for presenting them here is that, all together, these writings give a picture of some aspects of life in Southwest France during German occupation which, to a certain extent, must have remained a sealed book to the outside world.

As I consider the momentous events of these years, Meredith's famous Ode to France in 1870 appears even more applicable to the France of 1944.

Meredith's Ode to France

Soaring France!
Now is humanity on trial in thee:
Now mayest thou gather humankind in fee:
Now prove that reason is a quenchless scroll;
Make a calamity auriole:
And bleeding, head us through the troubles of the sea.

Chapter 1
Upheaval

Paris, Sunday 9 June 1940 – I set off to 11:00 o'clock Mass at the Madeleine – across the sun-chequered pavement under the green dome of the plane trees to the West Side door and up the narrow stairway past the dungeon-like Votive Chapel. It was thronged with silent worshippers standing or kneeling with heads bowed before its numerous shrines. As I climbed, the dank smell of candle-smoke gave way to the fragrant incense burnt during High Mass in the great church overhead. Whilst the ceremony proceeded, the vast temple was flooded by light from above. The Swiss, the silver-chained ushers, the altar-boys moved with a serenity befitting the Olympian precincts and an immutable rite of service. *Tu es Petrus* – here at least was something fixed amidst the general turmoil.

The atmosphere in Paris was becoming panicky – nervous and constrained since the one and only bombardment some weeks previously, tension was on the increase. The fashionable congregation had faded away. Gone were many well-known figures – perhaps having bolted to their provincial *châteaux*. The blue-robed, white-coiffed Little Sisters of the Poor were kneeling at the door as usual, for their mission of mercy would last to the end of time.

Out on the shady columned porch we stood for a few moments to gaze at the view. Whose eyes could resist plunging down the rue Royale and following the long line of perspective across the Seine to where, in the distance, the scintillating tones of gold, blue, green and brown of a glorious Parisian day, melted to restfulness?

Nearby, however, all was movement. The gait of worshippers, slow as they descended the long flight of steps, quickened once they reached the pavement. Newsboys were hawking *Paris-Midi* to eager buyers. Round the corner swung great lorry-loads of bicycles from the Gare

Saint Lazare. The stream of refugees constantly detraining from Rouen and the Oise valley stumbled pitifully past us towards an unknown destiny, fleeing to the South or West – anywhere indeed to escape the advancing Germans.

Along the Boulevard to the Place de l'Opéra, café fronts were already busy. It was the usual cosmopolitan mix – uniforms, stylish dresses, numerous Czechs and Poles, and the ubiquitous Spanish refugee. The Café de la Paix was crammed. Here I'd find American and English colleagues holding a brief news exchange over pre-prandial drinks, but I did not stop as I wanted to look in at the office before lunch. It was empty, typewriters covered, telephones quiet. The large room had been cleared of the previous night's litter of papers. Tables had been tidied, chairs stacked, dictionaries and reference books put away. A trim file of weekend papers awaited to be opened. There were no urgent telegrams, the post insignificant. As always, in emergencies, Printing House Square was leaving it to the man on the spot, a confidence I, for one, had always greatly appreciated. Off to lunch I went leaving the electric clock ticking away fateful half minutes and the tall mirror above the mantelpiece reflecting the map of tortured France. What indeed was happening to France?

My wife and I had lunch at Bernard's, which not only had the advantage of offering good food at reasonable prices but was also only a few steps away from No. 19 where, amidst the late Monsieur Réne Puaux's hellenistic treasures, we had a temporary home. We did not know it at the time but it was to be our last relaxing meal for many a year – excellent cooking, selection of meats, smooth wines, fragrant coffee, quiet service – carefree enjoyment, adieu!

There was an important conference to be attended that afternoon. The Minister of Propaganda wanted to see the Paris representatives of the foreign press at 6:00 pm. It was a difficult time of day for the Chief Correspondent to be absent from his desk, so I attended. Climbing the thickly-carpeted stairs under the gaze of the watchful gendarmes and walking the endless corridors of the old Hotel Continental, one caught glimpses of disordered rooms, papers pulled out of pigeon-holes and typewriters being packed. The Minister, a smooth-faced youngish man who had only recently reached the top of the ladder, greeted us genially but appeared little inclined to talk of the war. He told us he had been educated in England and so, he said, had special pleasure in clasping the hands of English colleagues. Keeping carefully to polite generalities, he expressed a desire to allow the Foreign Press as much latitude for comment as was compatible with present circumstances. "What the hell are the circumstances, I should like to know?" muttered one of the American press men. "Monsieur le Ministre, could you tell us if the government is preparing to leave Paris?" asked an English correspondent, pleading that journalists, though prepared to travel light and move quickly, also have arrangements to make when central offices must be abandoned.

There is no intention of leaving, he declared, assuring us that we would receive due notice as it was his earnest desire to keep in close touch with us. Nevertheless, at 11 a.m. next morning, our messenger, on taking a telegram to the Continental, was informed that the Censor's Office had moved to Tours, and that all despatches, other than spot news filed in Paris, would be forwarded to Tours by car in the afternoon for censorship. The War Office Staff Colonel, who had given military briefings every morning, had also taken French leave of our company. There would be no more grand meetings at the long table in the historic Salle des Armures.

So the government that was to have fought it out before Paris, or in Paris, had fled. My own impression that Reynaud's stomach for the fight would, in the end, prove no better than Negrin's, had been depressing me for some time, but it was now the accepted view. French resistance, or worse, her will to resist, was wilting – Gamelin's incompetence, Reynaud's pusillanimity, what next?

At the office, Cadett announced that he would have to race to Tours at once, normally a journey of about four hours via Orléans. He left. Soon it would be my turn. Our car had been garaged in Passy, from where, a few days earlier, in view of the wholesale requisitioning of cars – sign of impending exodus – I had brought it, for safety, to the courtyard of No. 19. After phoning my wife to urge her to start packing, I put in an afternoon at the office. I was alone. The typist had rushed off to Normandy to rescue his wife and child. The Commercial Department was closed, the staff having left; and the office boy had gone to Maisons-Laffitte to escape with his family on their bicycles. Successively I filed several messages at the telegraph Agency for local news. This was dull hopeless work which would be duplicated by every journalist still in town. These were sad but busy hours in the deserted office. One could sense that the scramble had begun and that the city was visibly emptying.

I went home for a scrappy meal and to help finish loading the car – not the easiest in the blackout. Sleeping with the window open one could hear, during fits of wakefulness, excited voices and bits of conversation rising from the passing stream of refugees.

Hoping to reach Tours for lunch we aimed to start shortly after 6:00 a.m., as dawn broke. Across the Place the gigantic colonnade of refugees loomed through a sooty fog. In the air was a smell reminiscent of Barcelona when the Italian bombers hit the oil tanks below Montjuïc and the city had been covered by a pall of smoke for several days. Oil was burning somewhere. Just after midnight there had been some violent bomb explosions North or Northwest of Paris and the heavy crump-crumping of a raid. So they had got something, or was it the French destroying stores? The concierge, stocky, red-faced, black-skirted, broom in hand, contributed another version: The Germans had crossed the Seine under cover of a smokescreen; the owner of the house had departed to her château near Nevers in a fast Bugatti; the other flats were closed; with us gone she would be alone, she quietly remarked, as if it were normal for concierges to remain to receive invaders.

It was just 7:00 a.m. by the Opéra clock when I pulled the heavily laden car to the curb and went up to have a last look in at the office. The only mail was a letter for one of the clerks in the Commercial Department, long before gone. Yesterday's litter of papers lay about. It struck me as odd that the concierge, whom I crossed on the stairs, dusting as usual, would be sweeping up the place to receive the Gestapo gents. Well, we had no secret archives to burn as at the Quai d'Orsay so the square-head myrmidons would find no ashes in the grate. How it had glowed every afternoon during the lonely Christmas and New Year that had been my initiation to the Paris office! The new radio set, what a pity to abandon it, and the dictionaries, who would be next to use them? On my desk lay P. Dehilotte's *Gestapo* with an inscribed dedication by the author. One imagined inquisitive eyes spying it; then perhaps the curse.

But there was no time to linger. When walking out I little realised that within ten days I would sacrifice a prized career and lose one of the most interesting jobs to which a journalist could aspire. In wartime, personal tragedies count as naught, alas! Mercilessly grind the wheels of circumstance.

Chapter 2
Flight

Back to the Madeleine once more, down the stately rue Royale, across the Place de la Concorde and along the riverbank – traffic was sparse and we sped along at a good pace. The Marines were gone from the Ministry on the Place but, behind the neighbouring cream façade of the United States Embassy, Bill Bullitt would be waiting for the grey-green hosts. Sturdy *percherons*[1] determinedly pulled vegetable carts towards the *Halles*. The neat bunches of carrots and turnips were the last sign of Parisian normality. Soon, doubtless, the horses would be pulling German waggons. Flowers tied with crèpe lay at the foot of the memorial to King Albert I. Most of the Belgians who had brought them in tribute a few days earlier would be joining the exodus.

Picked up Mundy, a marooned colleague pacing the paved courtyard of one of Paris's most modern blocks of flats. Thence across to the Avenue de Malakoff to collect Missonne, an invalid comrade of 1914–18. Having abandoned all they possessed, both found nooks for themselves between our stacks of luggage. We made our way along the boulevards des Maréchaux that ring Paris. Bomb craters near the Duke of Windsor's mansion. Before reaching the Porte d'Orléans, traffic police diverted us to the tourist road through the Valley of Chevreuse, with the main highways reserved for military traffic. Up the Seine a long procession of barges steamed incessantly, trying to escape by the back door of canals to the Loire or Rhone. As we mounted the heights beyond, the smoky atmosphere thinned and a glorious summer's day came into its own. Cars were coming in from every side and soon we were all locked together, a mere one in a despairing mass of crawling,

1. Carthorses.

stopping, crawling-again-only-to-stop-again vehicles, from which there was no escape. Sometimes the column would get up enough speed for second gear but it was mostly a case of grinding in first with a foot or so separating vehicles in front and behind. Vans, luxury limousines, cars large and small of every type, make and age, jumbled together by fate. It was no wild medley, however exasperating the pace and maddening the frequent halts. No impatient honking. Progress consisted of a succession of violent jerks despite which there was little bumping – a singular tribute to the average skill of the French driver. Many cars had mattresses and furniture strapped on the roofs. Some were crammed with a jumble of odds and ends – children's toys and draught boards, the family canary, cat and dog, canoes and bicycles galore. An infant, cradled in a wheelbarrow tied behind a cart, slept peacefully despite the jolting and noise. There were weather-stained cars from Holland, Belgium and the North, which had been on the road for days and whose occupants, now having left the area of military operations with its bombing and machine-gunning, were taking the exodus calmly. They had no specific destination, trundling along in the hands of fate, glad that immediate danger was past. How quickly resilience asserts itself and people accept having to live from hand to mouth! But most of us, anxious to get ahead, apply ourselves to threading a way through the maze – heart-breaking work, only gaining at most a few hundred yards for hours of effort, but a manner of working off pent-up energy.

A signpost pointing backwards read: Versailles 25 kilometres. We had been on the road nearly nine hours and were still within walking distance of Paris. Tours seemed distantly remote. Then a piece of good luck – a couple of planes, swastikas clearly visible, came wheeling overhead. The column halted and people flung themselves into neighbouring cornfields. "If only I had a gun", our grizzled veteran groaned. They soon left us but we heard their bombs and saw smoke rising from a village in the direction of Chartres. Then came a great honking from the rear. Several light lorries and cars, bearing French Air Force markings, came along, bumping and swaying, half on the road, half in the fields. It was an opportunity to pull out and, keeping behind the airmen, to get to the head of the column. We were free at last, but only for a spell.

Nightfall overtook us, jammed in an interminable village, with cars parked everywhere. Suddenly came anguished cries for help from a man calling out that his wife was about to have a baby. Willing hands helped to move his car out of the ruck. A little later, my wife got out of our car and walked up a narrow, cobbled alley, feeling sick and dizzy. A kindly woman, seeing her plight, brought her a chair and then took us into her cottage and offered a bed in the loft. I went back to drive the car out of the village, in view of an early start the following morning. Our two passengers proposed to keep an eye on the car and to sleep on the grass next to it.

I returned to join my wife, managing to get some cheese, bread and wine on the way. We sat in the kitchen, ate and talked awhile. This deluge has been upon us for the last three days, said our hostess, who appeared to consider France's tragedy a scourge sent by the Almighty. Something was obviously very wrong, she went on, with girls only thinking of hair-waves, lipsticks and the cinema. She had for years kept a little shop after first earning her living as an umbrella repairer. She had married a gardener – the old man and his dog were dozing in the corner. "He will be off at dawn as usual", said his wife. Her daughter was eager to be a schoolteacher and was studying at Tours. A son of fourteen helped his father and the other son was in the Aviation Corps. This war is not like the last, continued the woman; then there was a spirit, now lacking. "Clemenceau and Poincaré, they were true men." Of course she was right, a hundred thousand times right, this humble woman so firmly settled in her stone-built house in the village side-street. With it, plus garden, and a patch of vines, she counted herself happy and content. The children might go out into a changing and seemingly somewhat subversive world but she herself had no ambitions beyond her home. Were the Germans coming, she asked. In 1870 they had passed through the village but at Châteaudun had been stopped in a fierce battle, high watermark of the invasion. Would they get further this time after the second Sédan? The word rang like a knell.

Next morning we were off early, with a present of fresh strawberries to remind us of the little garden at Bonneval. At Châteaudun we found another fierce jam. Cast-iron shells lay piled up at a foundry. Would they ever be used? At Vendôme we were stuck once more, but only 30 miles to go. The broad highway stretched before us as we left the crowded town but the traffic police pushed us onto a side road once again. These were fairly clear except when we came upon villages with cars thick as flies around them. Petrol was running low when, opportunely, we espied English soldiers near a wood. They were RAF men. We pulled up and soon negotiated a tin of petrol which the car, sheltering behind a bush, ingurgitated through a funnel improvised with the last number of The Times we were to see for many a long day. Some miles further on, stopped for lunch at a little village outside Amboise. It was full of French airmen, among whom Missonne found an acquaintance who gave us the news – no change, the retreat continued. We crossed the Loire at Amboise, little thinking that in a few days French Plenipotentiaries for an Armistice would be meeting the Germans there. Then the Cher and at last we arrived at Tours from the South.

The place was a seething mass of cars. Found Cadett but he had not been able to retain rooms so I set out in search of a billet. Finally fetched up at a Doctor's Clinique where we were able to park in the courtyard. Rubber mattressed bed. Then off to work in an attic with painters frantically attempting to turn a tumble-down mill into a Censor's office with some semblance of decency. The only furniture was some narrow school benches and desks, much carved by generations of young boys and highly polished by elbows and breeches. Recording cars were packed in the muddy yard. On rickety stairs and in tortuous streets I met colleagues from Spain. The World Press seemed concentrated in Tours. Outside, at Candey, in the heart of beautiful Châteaux country, fate was holding court, but the echoes of supreme decisions never reached the end of the wires we served. Between stood the Censor.

Tours was literally crammed. A vast army of government hangers-on of every description and both sexes clogged the hotels; a multitude thronged the streets. In the narrow rue des Halles was a little restaurant-bar run by Spanish refugees who toiled to feed clamouring waves of customers. Curious turn of fate bringing beggared stragglers from Madrid, Valencia and Barcelona to reap a fortune from fleeing French. At nightfall, over congested Tours, came the menace of hostile aircraft. Blackout sketchy. Also a moon. Important bridges North and South of the railway station offered legitimate targets. Just before dusk, highflung bursts of A.A., directed apparently against reconnaissance planes, spread alarm. Later, violent firing, the crump of bomb bursts and shrieks in the courtyard, brought the household to the ground floor. The Concierge was throwing a fit. Her little granddaughter, aged about 10, was quite calm. She showed us to the cellar and we dragged her wailing granny into it. Suddenly a drum-fire of bomb-bursts shook the place. They must be going for the bridges, we thought; later we heard Tours aerodrome was the object of the attack.

Many cars began leaving Tours next morning. "Government moving to Bordeaux", the Censor informed us. And so the great trek resumed in much the same conditions as the rush from Paris, except that we were allowed to use the main road. Inhabitants were leaving on foot. Seven nuns in grey habits and voluminous coiffes, carrying rolled blankets, marched along behind their Mother Superior. Every town and village was blocked with queues around petrol pumps, most of them empty. At Angoulême, after a long wait, we managed to fill up, but nightfall was near. To avoid exasperating congestion in towns, we resolved to camp up a side road. Stopped at a crossroads where there was a farm. Kindly, the peasant owners watering their beasts invited us to use their kitchen and sleep in the spare bed in the attic. A look at the bed and we begged for some straw in the barn, saying we would have more room there and be less of a nuisance to the household. A goat was moved out lest her munching disturb us. Bringing clean sheets from the car, we settled in comfortably enough. As we partook of a scrappy supper in the kitchen, conversation turned to the war. As normal, their sons had signed up. France had a powerful ally in England. Why had the front collapsed? Were the Germans coming? How far behind us were they? Why was everybody abandoning their homes? Questions impossible to answer when, in the absence of resolute leadership, the truth was indeed what the sturdy farmers already sensed: France was slipping towards catastrophe. The smiling countryside with its livestock, crops, vines; everything would become the booty of a ruthless enemy. No foreigners in arms had trod these soils since the days of the Black Prince. Now the Boche was at the door. We left the family in tribulation, discussing the problems our forebears faced when the Saracens marched towards their doom at Poitiers – should they drive their livestock into the woods? Oh for a Charles Martel!

Lying in the straw of the barn, listening to mice rustling, two pictures of the long day's events kept recurring. One was of a railway embankment barring the road far on either side. A regiment of Annamites, stationed somewhere near, had come out to face the foe. With great industry they had erected strong-points, abattis, chevaux-de-frise – every textbook obstacle to delay the enemy's advance. Right in the bottleneck constituted by the hole in the embankment through which the road passed, flanked by the stone bastions of an overhead bridge, farm implements were piled cunningly so that only one car at a time could negotiate the passage by describing a double S. The Colonel himself, a wizened colonial in calico khaki, riding-whip in hand, stood at the entrance to this maze, surrounded by his smiling men. As a joke on the impatient, impenitent invaders, it was splendid; but was it a joke or another sign of the incompetence that helped make the chaotic flight still more disastrous! A few piled harrows, surrounded by amused colonial troops, to stop the Panzers – had France really come to that?

The other picture was of a stopped car and two men quietly pacing up and down, smoking and gesticulating. One was a sturdy figure in black. Dr. Negrin was sharing with us the flight from Paris just as we had shared his from Madrid and Barcelona.

Next morning broke gloriously. The fragrance of the sunny South beckoned. It was Sunday. The road was clear. As we sped along, bells ringing for mass called from a village steeple. There was no altar-boy. An old woman gave the responses from the body of the church. The little village shrine, just like the *Madeleine,* offered a haven and anchorage. *Oh, La Madeleine!* Already the clumping boots of enemy soldiers would be stomping down its majestic aisle.

As we neared Bordeaux, we crossed giant tankers driving north, carrying petrol to marooned vehicles. We then made our way over the long, narrow stone bridge, the great city's one and only road communication across the broad river. Streets and squares were crowded with the bedraggled mobs whose flight had done so much to cause chaos and demoralise the nation. Mingled with them were genuine refugees – Czechs and Poles, joined by British from all over southern France, preparing to leave the country.

Since Mundy had left us at Tours to try and reach England via Nantes, we picked up another passenger, a plucky French girl chauffeuring some elderly Polish ladies to the South. Their car had broken down near the farm where we spent the night. She hoped to get another car at Bordeaux to rescue them. Cauderan was her destination so we took her there and, as the centre of Bordeaux was so hopelessly overcrowded, we sought a billet for ourselves in that suburb. A retired ship's purser took us in. His cool, tile-floored rooms and peach-filled garden are peaceful memories of those hectic days.

Chapter 3
Armistice de Malheur

In Bordeaux it was soon apparent that no new Charles Martel would spring from the vineyards of the Gironde. Nor in that sea of confusion did there appear to be anyone decided on anything except to float, however uncomfortably, along the river of least resistance towards surrender. The inner rottenness of France's parliamentary and political regime became fully apparent. In the emergency, now acute, there were those who affirmed that nothing could be done without consulting *Les Chambres*. These were composed not so much of representatives of the people as of the spineless pleasure seekers and preying oligarchies a too prosperous France had bred. No Gambetta appeared to rouse the innate patriotism one felt must somewhere lie dormant. Instead there was Laval and the defeatist clique whose smooth tongues were hard at work in the dubious atmosphere of hotel and café. Reynaud and Mandel were proving mere playthings of fate without sufficient strength of character to make any difference. The tearful wing-clipped President was of no calibre and in no position, even if he had wished it, to make history.

Such was the pass to which decadence under the Third Republic had brought a proud nation. Yet the Republic, served by other men, had steered the country to victory through the terrible ordeal of 1914–18. By a supreme irony of destiny, it was one of those steadfast leaders, the man whose name was eternally linked with an indomitable feat of resistance, Pétain of Verdun, who became the apostle of surrender. Old *On-ne-passe-pas* was ready, it appeared, to throw in his hand. Nearly a quarter of a century had passed. The 84 year old, recalled from his Embassy in Spain, found himself in the same position as Weygand – consulted too late. Weygand's responsibilities as Commander-in-Chief were purely military. He had, in fact, reported that the French

Army, broken, outnumbered, and outclassed in armament, could no longer be counted upon as a supreme argument in national policy. It would fight the enemy to the last, if ordered, but the struggle would be useless. Enough had been done to save France's honour. This terrible message from Foch's right-hand, pronounced in the gardens of Touraine, became a dire portent. For many Frenchmen who had no idea how the campaign was going, nor who had yet realised the supremacy tanks and aircraft had established in modern warfare, it was a bolt from the blue. Kept secret at first, it leaked out in Bordeaux and spread consternation. Pétain accepted it.

The stress laid upon the men in office by the terrible situation in which France found itself preyed upon them. The weaker turned to the stronger and there stood Pétain, with his reputation for steadfastness, ready to take the most fearsome responsibilities. In the last resort what more presentable figure than *le dernier Maréchal de France* to obtain from the Germans any terms still negotiable? Who to be a better judge of what France's honour demanded than the glorious soldier?

There was a previous question to decide, however. Might it not be in France's best interest to give up the struggle on metropolitan soil and continue the war from Algeria, based on the Empire. The three Departments there were, in every respect but the geographical, an extension of France herself. France's alliances would be preserved, communications with America maintained by the fleet and the manpower of France's immense African Dominions could be drawn upon. Apart from the recent action of King Haakon and Queen Wilhelmina there was no other precedent in modern European history since the disastrous retreat of the Serbians in 1914 and the headlong flight of King John of Portugal to Brazil when Marshal Junot's ragged troops appeared outside Lisbon in 1807. It meant a heroic plunge into the unknown for which, indeed, the Nation had no stomach.

Following Churchill's dogged intimation that whatever France might do, England would fight on, it required a breadth of view, which few in Bordeaux possessed, to visualise the possibilities of what might appear an act of desperation. Moreover, the idea that Government should depart was naturally anathema to the host of hangers-on threatened with desertion. Unfortunately, Pétain's upbringing was that of a soldier not statesman – his the narrower view. Since the "Council of Ministers and Lamentations" held in Paris on May 27, when the capitulation of the Belgian Army and of the King became known, and during which General Weygand had said the battle was lost, the majority of the Cabinet was persuaded that there was nothing left but to seek an Armistice. Pétain was with them, apparently hoping that an Armistice would halt the Germans in their tracks and save territory from occupation. Every step forward by the German columns into the heart of France increased the Marshal's desire to negotiate; the only way left open, as he saw it, of serving France's interests. The Marshal had no axe to grind. In this respect he stood in the eyes of the people high above the political class. He was trusted, they were not. No one dared doubt Pétain's patriotism. Hence his unquestionable ascendancy and their acceptance of him as their guide in this darkest hour.

It remains to be seen whether the Marshal's contact with the *Munichois* and *Défaitistes* will go down in history as the personal tragedy of Philippe Pétain as well as of France. It may be that his was too narrow a view, that the mind of the octogenarian had not developed as rapidly as the French Empire itself in that he could not conceive of a Greater France beyond French soil. For him France centred in the old tower in Flanders where he was born and in the sunlit olive grove in Provence he had selected for his residence in retirement and ultimate resting place.

Of course, the situation was not as clear then as one sees it now in retrospect, but the elements of tragedy were obvious enough and doom hung in the air. However it may have been, as the world's pressmen burrowed incessantly, they bared the skeleton in the cupboard into startling nakedness. It was despairing to discover so much of which so little could be said. Despite the mass of detail and long hours spent threshing about the teeming town, work seemed pointless, so true is it that only in freedom can a journalist's pen flow to full purpose.

Bordeaux is a city of wide avenues, broad squares, interminable quays. Yet it was all too small for the multitudes that thronged it, awaiting events. Many families drove off towards the Basque country or the Pyrenees, but as many, and more, continued to flood in. The broad Gironde was crowded with shipping. Embarkation Officers were hard at work helping British subjects; holiday seekers who had come to France despite the war, residents from Pau and elsewhere responding to warnings issued by the British Embassy. The Consulates of Spain and Portugal were besieged day and night by wealthy central Europeans, many of them Jews, Austrians and Czechs who during the past two years had drifted to the South of France and were now in danger of being trapped unless they could pass the Pyrenees. The Poles had left their Headquarters at Angers; Czechs and Belgians were hurrying from Montpellier and Narbonne. The pre-Armistice clear-out was progressing by the hour.

Amidst everything else, we had, of course, to find sustenance. Squeezed four at a tiny table in a restaurant, we found it difficult to eat while customers encumbered passage-ways, impeding the service despite the clatter and laughter that always accompanies mealtimes in the Midi when, whatever the food, the certainty of a *bonne bouteille* is there to cheer. Suddenly, the couple opposite, middle-aged well-dressed foreigners, dissolved into tears. While my wife tried to comfort the lady, the man explained their woes. Refugees from Czechoslovakia, after much travelling he had found a billet as an Engineer in the North of France. Now they were homeless once more and, to boot, separated from their children. Would they find their children in time to get away before the Germans arrived? To get away! The major worry of thousands. At the British Consulate where Embarkation Officers worked tirelessly, families implored in vain, some pitifully even on their knees. "British first" was the order, which was quite natural.

The British Embassy was housed in one of the old fashioned hotels with a vast hall as full of old furniture as an antiquary's shop. Even here conversation would become heated though not so much as in another establishment peremptorily closed by the military authority as a centre of conspiracy.

British Press Correspondents had a short, if interesting, spell of work. Hardly had they been two days in Bordeaux when the order came to embark at Le Verdon. The censorship had been set up in what seemed a hastily cleared hairdresser's establishment on the first floor of an old house near the Exchange. The premises, though central, were far too small. Here, in an atmosphere of cheerful togetherness, correspondents typed the last brief messages of a momentous campaign.

On the broad square, the Pressmen's caravan was gathering. Powerful, battered cars of the "Specials" contrasted with the sleek limousines of the resident correspondents from Paris, carrying their families. For these, most of whom had spent the best part of their lives in the French capital, return to their own country spelt the loss of their homes. Sadness could be read in many faces at the sudden ending of a chapter in their lives. But the Special Correspondents were eager to be off, already anticipating new adventures. In high spirits, they called to each other and headed off toward café fronts for a last drink. In and out among the crowds strolled fezzed Algerians hawking chamois cloths and feather dusters while superior, black-coated gentlemen did a brisk business buying cars for cash – cars which, perforce, would be abandoned at the quayside. Towards midday, as the sun gathered strength, cars drew out from under the trees, bumped over the curb and the column set off. Friends waved and answering toots came from the motor-horns. The British Press had departed.

Were the British Correspondents recalled or sent away? In truth, they did not know but all realised that the Franco-British Alliance, keystone of world politics, was crumbling. They who had loyally served it, chronicling alike triumphs and misfortunes, would at least be spared the bitterness of witnessing its final demise. Among the friends of France who departed were men who felt that the Alliance, whatever the appearances, was too deep-rooted to die on command. Among the friends of England who regretfully waved them farewell were many, similarly devoted to the cause of honour and Christian civilisation for which the Alliance stood.

For some days after the departure of the Press Correspondents, the British Embassy lingered at Bordeaux. The hasty embarkation of British subjects and diverse refugees was transferred to Bayonne and St. Jean de Luz. The censorship moved from the barber's shop to a magnificent modern Trade Union headquarters building on the outer boulevard. A new staff took charge, first sign of the coming change in the political régime. Mr Alexander, First Lord of the Admiralty, came to take cognizance of the proposed Armistice terms concerning the French Fleet. His disapproval of them sowed the seed for the disaster at Mers-el-Kébir, first blood shed between the two Nations since Waterloo.

After the departure of the journalists I had hoped to be able to continue corresponding with Printing House Square for some time. To do so usefully I had to keep in contact with the British Embassy so long as it remained in Bordeaux. This proved impossible, for when I called to see a High Official with whom I was personally acquainted, and although standing only a few yards away when my card was handed to him, he turned a glassy eye on me and my request. Not one word. As he moved away I felt the veil of distrust descending, destined to cloud the outlook between English and French.

There was also a lesson to learn at the Censorship. Under the new regime, interpretation was barred. Henceforth the news-bell would give only one sound. Nothing but the official version of events had any chance of getting through. In these circumstances I could no longer hope to be of any service to *The Times*. My self-set mission collapsed.

That night I took to the road again, free from all immediate duties. As we sped along the great highway through a hundred miles of balmy pine forests, there was none of the elation that used to come as the miles ticked away leading homewards from tragic scenes in Spain. Instead, a leaden feeling of bondage, foreboding of coming years of covert shame, outright humiliation and servitude.

We left Bordeaux at 9 p.m. and reached Biarritz before midnight. The last hour of the journey was brightened by the chatter of an irrepressible youth making for Bayonne.

Biarritz was a hive of activity, the weather glorious, the beaches crowded. The most irresponsible and apparently wealthiest refugees from three nations had found their haven. Rows of shining cars were parked all around the big hotels. Cocktails, frivolity, revelry in the restaurants and night clubs, carefree life on the beach, were the order of the day. In fairness to the French, most of the revellers seemed to be foreigners – Dutch, American and Belgians.

The large British Colony had divided loyalties. For many of them France was a second homeland. They could hardly imagine any harm coming to them where they had lived, some of them for over half a century. Many of the elderly chose to remain. Perhaps they thought their age would protect them, poor things. Those who, in response to Consular warnings, decided to go, had two routes open – to take passage on the crowded refugee ships or to go to Spain or Portugal.

Obtaining necessary visas at the under-staffed, over-crowded Consulates was a terrible business. With the last of my petrol, I brought an English friend, anxious to get his young family away, to Hendaye, where he hoped the Spanish Consul would be more accessible than at Bayonne. They had failed to board an over-crowded ship at Bayonne after waiting many hours at the quayside, so had reverted to their original idea of seeking refuge in Spain. We took the coast road. Since I had last been along it six months previously, barriers had been erected and tank traps dug, facing South. The enemy, however, was approaching from the North! A long row of cars waited outside the Consulate on the bank of the estuary of the Bidassoa, in full view of the magnificent panorama of Spanish sierras, crowned by the Trois Couronnes. How near Spain seemed and yet how remote! What a contrast the peace of those sunlit uplands with the human anguish down below. It was not on the view, however, that the gaze of the occupants of the cars was fixed but on a door guarded by a *gendarme*. An Englishman and his wife told us they had been waiting two days and nights in the queue.

On hearing this, my friend changed his plans once again. We had seen a large liner, in all probability a rescue ship, anchored in St. Jean de Luz, so we hurried back. In effect the ship, the *Arandora Star*, was to take Poles, Czechs and the remaining British the following day.

That night there was a wild scramble; many plans were revised, thanks to the big ship and the confidence she inspired.

In the few crucial days preceding the Armistice, historians will find the most confused period in modern French history. They will have the task of discovering who really, for better or worse, was directing affairs; the Government or the Government in waiting; and whether or not, as was whispered, a *coup d'état* had covertly been effected. While this supreme struggle was taking place between rival groups, the French people lay prostrate – propitiatory victim, if ever there was one, of cruel circumstance. Armed resistance had practically ceased and the Panzer divisions, reeling East and South, reached the Swiss frontier and into the Rhone Valley. In only one direction, the southwest, was their march stayed, doubtless by order.

While the British Embassy was still in Bordeaux, the Germans made one savage air raid on that crowded city, laying a trail of death across it. The population, stunned like the rest of France, in sonambulesque fashion, picked up its wounded and buried the dead.

At last, the tension with which French men and women awaited the worst was broken by a quavering voice that seemed to issue from the grave. For an interminable quarter of an hour it struggled on, sounding to many listeners an echo of despair. The bars of *La Marseillaise* that followed were sheer mockery, trumpeting *"Le jour de gloire est arrivé"*. Instead of the immortal rallying cry "*aux armes, citoyens*", what they really chanted was "*sans armes, citoyens*". Regiments were disbanding, not marshalling. Roland Dorgelès, in a recent number of *Gringoire,* gave a sense of the oppression of defeat that weighed down Frenchmen when the *Armistice de Malheur* sounded on 25 June. As the *Goncourt* academician put it: "Hope that day lay buried. Surrender. Set teeth. In vain to stiffen. For the obsession that all was lost ground in. Vanished all that one loved and possessed. Only the horrible feeling of being half man, half a Frenchman. The dreadful malady leading to amputation had lasted only a month after twenty years of incubation. How hard to end one's days in the skin of defeat.

The sun shone bright but hope was dead. What a contrast to the dull sky but bright hopes of 11 November, twenty-two years previously. Sitting beside the silent wireless set – for after the Marshal's fateful message, who could bear to hear more? – one's thoughts, as if unconsciously seeking relief, reverted to the other armistice and the many memories of that crowded hour when long-deferred hopes spilled over and pent-up emotion broke loose. We'd seen many a muddy road in Flanders, sodden fields, dripping trees, brimful ditches and great craters at cross-roads, blown up by retreating Germans. At one of these a crucifix – one of the many large wooden images set up in this religious country – had been tipped forward by an explosion so that the Crucified appeared to be peering through the crevices at His feet into the depths below. On the thorn-crowned Head, a German helmet had been placed and from each nail-pierced Hand hung a stick-bomb – the Hun's idea of a joke, perpetrated in retreat. Now the barbarians had returned triumphant and France acknowledged defeat.

Chapter 4

Harsh Reality

France, though stunned, shocked, and sickened, did not long remain comatose. Beneath the bowed head the body moved, the blood too hot to be chilled. There is more of a stubborn element in the Northern and Eastern populations than can be cowed; too much Latin exuberance in the South to lie motionless; plenty of resilience in the adventure-tried Normans, Bretons, and Basques. Thus, a train of events was set in motion because, being the great political and ethnological composite that it is, nothing in France can rest still for long.

The magnificent rallying-call of General de Gaulle greatly raised spirits and ignited the flame of hope. "*La Guerre n'est pas finie*" became the phrase of the moment and remained the watchword, especially for the less well-off classes. It was balm to wounded pride to feel that, somewhere, soldiers fighting under the French flag were in action against the hereditary enemy. The Croix de Lorraine was a happy augury, for Joan of Arc is the purest and most popular of the legion of heroic figures thrown up in French history. German attempts to exploit the pyre on the marketplace at Rouen failed miserably. People thought of the smoke of June 1940, not of that of May 1431.

Nevertheless, the chances and means of escape were so limited, and the difficulties so many, that only a symbolic force of Frenchmen succeeded in getting away. Inevitably, the great mass remained on French soil to face defeat and its calamitous consequences. Oh! the anguish of that black, though beautiful, summer when a broken people came face-to-face with cruel destiny! The Armistice brought the mad exodus to an end, leaving no less than ten million refugees, a quarter of the population of the country, to make their way back to their homes. A few, tempted by the gorgeous weather and obeying the light-hearted reflex to the signal "immediate danger passed", dallied awhile, camping by seaside or forest, but were soon disillusioned by stark reality as the shadow of difficulties ahead dawned on them. In truth, for a while the speed of the fall veiled the depth to which France had fallen.

To get home! That was the first problem and indeed a serious one in view of the lack of petrol, disruption of road and rail transport, and not least the barrier from Switzerland to the Pyrenees raised overnight by the fatidic line of demarcation, representing the new frontier between occupied and unoccupied France. Across that barrier nobody might pass, and what is more important for the life of a country whose economy must function or have its people perish, nothing could pass without the consent of the Occupying Power. This was the euphemistic name by which the Germans were referred to in an effort to tone down the irritating effect the word *Allemand* had on all French ears. Although nominally still administered by their own authorities, for the average French man and woman local life was soon controlled at every turn by the rules dictated by the *Kommandanturs*, with whose orders the administrative services were sternly enjoined by Article 3 of the Armistice to "collaborate in a correct manner". These rules grew like weeds on every side, hampering commerce and starving the population. Freedom was a thing of the past. Across significant parts of the country the blackout remained in force, if anything even more so than before.

Furthermore, to get home was one thing, to reconstitute the home quite another. Many lay literally in ruins where Panzers and dive-bombers had passed. More numerous were those where ruin came through the absence of the bread-winner, most likely now a prisoner, or through loss of employment given the changing economic conditions.

So the French came to learn what surrender meant. Perhaps the first and cruellest disillusionment came when the soldiers didn't return. For days, in countless homes, husband or father, son or brother, was eagerly awaited. The "at any moment he will be here" feeling lasted for weeks, but generally the "hope deferred maketh the heart sick" period ended piteously with a card or message from some camp in Germany or France. Being a prisoner in France seemed preposterous but indeed it was so for hundreds of thousands. And surrender did not save the two million ultimately marched off to Germany.

Sadly, divided families took stock whilst their loved ones began the long calvary towards the living death of the camps. For young men full of life and energy, to be prisoners of war must be one of the saddest of fates, although while one's country fights on there is always the sustaining hope of victory as well as motive for pride and dignity. Prisoners held as hostages of a defeated country must indeed be the most miserable of captives. Theirs is abject bondage, pure and simple – surely the greatest fall a man can endure.

Poor Jacques! One remembers him burly, red-headed, bursting with ardour. Mobilized in the South of France, after seven applications he succeeded in getting to the front in the "*drôle de guerre*"[2] during which there were at first too many soldiers and too little for them to do.

Captain in a battalion of volunteers, he arrived in time to take part in the skirmishing around Paris under a Governor who fled to Arcachon but was nonetheless subsequently decorated by Vichy. Lightly-trained forces like those of Jacques and his comrades could do little to parry the powerful thrusts of the Panzers. Back they went, from the Marne to the Seine, the Seine to the Loire, which they had no option but to swim across. One fine morning, on seeking orders at Headquarters, he found a notice saying that, to avoid encirclement, the general and his staff had moved on. Who could have confidence in such leaders? *Sauve qui peut.* Whilst the remnants of Jacques' unit dispersed, he himself and several comrades walked on southwards across country, doing their best to avoid the Germans.

Three days after the Armistice, whilst hiding in a wood on the edge of the unoccupied zone, they were discovered by a party of Germans hunting rabbits. What an ignominious end to the dash for freedom! The last his family saw of him was when his sister, making her way to Orléans, caught a glimpse of him through a prison window.

2. Literally the "Phoney War" – the eight month period before the invasion of France during which no fighting took place.

Unilateral interpretation of Article 4 of the Armistice provided that French forces, finding themselves in the zone to be occupied by Germany, should be withdrawn to unoccupied territory, there to be demobilised. In practice, however, there was to be no such withdrawal if the Germans could help it!

The Armistice was meant to come into effect at 1.30 a.m. on the night of 24 to 25 June. It was so little recognised by many commanders that, on 27 June, the division to which Ignace belonged was still fighting East of Montmédy. Ignace received his wound that day. Two days later, on repeated assurances from the German command as to the terms of the Armistice, the obstinate Divisional Commander surrendered. Despite this, he and his men, and a neighbouring division as well, were marched off to Germany.

Ignace's wound, over which he was at first inconsolable – *"quelle guigne, être blessé la guerre finie"*[3] – proved a blessing in disguise for on the strength of it he was exchanged after six months in a German hospital. Thus the flower of French manhood was marched away, human merchandise to be enslaved and haggled over for years. Were left the elderly, the women, the children, in a country divided in spirit, destined to be pillaged and starved each week more ruthlessly by the hated invader.

The occupation took place without spectacular violence, apart the ever-present threat of those clattering armoured cars and well-oiled guns. The troops remained disciplined and orderly. But the calm appropriation, day-by-day, month after month, of everything the Germans required, or merely desired, with the assistance of the nominal authorities at Vichy, proved to the French inhabitants of occupied territory how utterly abandoned they were. True, it was all very correct! The Germans presented bread and meat tickets when eating outside barracks and messes, but the tickets only cost them the paper on which they were printed, if indeed, like the rest, it had not been commandeered. The arbitrary fixation of the exchange rate, at one mark for twenty

3. What bad luck, to be wounded, the war being over.

francs, gave the German soldier an undreamt-of purchasing power. The ancient Huns had sacked Rome; their present-day counterparts contented themselves with buying up France for paper. For several months the Germans revelled in *café au lait* and *croissants,* four-course restaurant meals for less than a mark, wines and liqueurs *ad-lib.* What a country, they thought; what hogs, thought the French.

While this lasted, Hitler paraded in Paris and Goering took possession of Jeanneney's luxurious apartment in the Luxembourg district. Stomachs were stuffed, the big shops rifled, but most important of all, England was not beaten. From Paris down to the smallest hamlet, all the stocks in the shops, from silk stockings to carpenters' tools, disappeared in post parcels to the "Vaterland".

Humiliation accompanied organised "legal" robbery. Before markets opened in the morning and while the townspeople queued outside closed doors, the Germans were allowed in to take their pick. Such were the inconsiderate and irritating orders of the *Kommandanturs.* Germans, civilian and military, were also allowed to travel free by rail and tram.

Countless incidents showed the utter disregard of the victors for the vanquished despite the soft soap of propaganda and oft-proclaimed generosity. I remember once in the Spring of 1941, when the first severe food shortage was being felt and even vegetables were scarce in the normally abundant Southwest, and the usual queue of women, old men and children was lined up outside a greengrocer's. Nearby were some German army horses, all in magnificent condition, bursting their lustrous coats. The awaited carrots arrived. The queue's listlessness disappeared, with distribution in sight. But a German quartermaster stepped forward and purchased the bulk of the greengrocer's parcel. Soon the horses were contentedly munching while the housewives departed, mostly empty-handed. If looks could kill! I should be glad of a horse beefsteak, murmured a girl; and I a slice of the sergeant's buttock, growled one of the tottering old men.

Another memory is *Goyesque.* It was one of those bitter days that can afflict the Côte d'Argent. The ever-prevailing humidity that makes it so green under a normally genial sun is freezing, freezing in one's bones, so penetrating it seems. Dusk is falling. Beneath the granite wall of the gas works, a German wagon is drawn up and its contents, a couple of tons of frozen potatoes, tipped out on the pavement. Amidst the icy slime and black mud, women and children search for still edible remnants. Clad in rags, their pallid faces blackened where dirty fingers have tried to pull tattered shawls closer over their heads, they poke and grope. Silence broods over the murky scene, except when the pain of hands or feet draws a cry.

The windows in the tavern across the way remain unlit. Only empty wine shops, empty stomachs, empty streets along which a starved dog prowls. This is Biarritz, bright, brilliant Biarritz, its now-empty market place, once overflowing with poultry, game, fish and fruit, together with the vegetable, groceries and wines that made France's name famous.

While the women and children toiled, the German soldiers looked on, hands in pockets, smoking contentedly. In their heavy jackboots, thick long-sleeved greatcoats, well-nourished, billeted in centrally-heated hotels, they felt not the cold. At most it stimulated appetites that would be satisfied at dinner-hour and it certainly was not draining away irreplaceable calories.

The cold of the winter of 1941–42 will not easily be forgotten. There was more fuel than ever before piled in the yards along the Adour but it was kept for the Germans and their requirements. The allowance of coal for a family of five was one sack of 50 kilogrammes for the whole winter. Next door to us stood a villa owned by a British subject and which was commandeered for a German officer. A lorry-load of coal was delivered and the caretaker ordered to stoke the furnace night and day for a week before the officer arrived. Then oak logs were brought in so the Major might enjoy the additional cheer of an open hearth. He lived alone with a dog, an Alsatian wolfhound, took all his meals out and was gone every morning by 8.30 a.m. Doubtless as exemplary and hard-working an officer as ever commanded a Flak company but nevertheless what a scandal of perishing locals alongside the empty house that is warm inside. In the early spring of 1942 officer and dog suddenly departed; rumour said to Russia. One cannot help hoping that he got there in time to feel a real touch of cold.

As the dreary months passed and the Pétain Government dallied with "*collaboration*", the French people saw normal life, as they knew it, wither; saw the wealth of France shrivel and the vaunted generosity of the victors exhibited only in scenes such as that of the Biarritz market. Suffering in spirit from humiliation, anger and distrust, in body from progressive malnutrition with its many accompanying ills, France learnt what misery really meant!

More than anything else perhaps, humiliation was ground in by the stamp, stamp of jackboots and the voice of the victors in song. German troops on the march have no spring; they lumber by, their step a heavy, endless thumping, a would-be knell of doom. The clump, clump, clump sounded day after day, night upon night, as sullen patrols passed up and down. Would it ever cease! And the singing! It was not tuneless; German voices rarely are, but it was remorseless. Nazi war songs, with one noteworthy exception, are defiant and troops must sing while passing through built-up areas. A curt order is barked; then the bawling follows, strident, staccato, insistent. No carefree song indeed but an ever-present reminder of relentlessness. There was no getting away from those two sounds, the stamp, stamp and the bawling.

Chapter 5
Privation

In contrast with the rapid military and political collapse, the subsequent long drawn-out agony of the French people was like a creeping paralysis extending insidiously into every household. Under the stress of privation and hunger, faculties dimmed and strength ebbed as energy was consumed in the incessant struggle. Frustration became the dominant, deceiving, demoralising factor as one difficulty inevitably led to another and families struggled to keep up their former standard of living. At first, rather than giving up the idea, say, of washing one's face without a sponge, one would search the town, shop-by-shop, and even extend the search to neighbouring towns – all in vain. Such peregrinations wore out one's shoes, even the shabbiest of which soon became precious possessions. Nor could one compensate for shabbiness by an extra polish, for shoe cream was one of the first articles to disappear. Galoshes and gumboots became irreplaceable. Those who could boast a pair became the envy of the town. Along the muddy road to *Hasparren*[4] a peasant splashed, sporting new rubber *sabots* (former price at any bazaar in Bayonne, 35 francs). "I had to give 6 dozen eggs for these", said he ruefully, because, within six months of the Armistice, eggs fetched anything up to 80 francs a dozen.

The lack of soap led to increased doses of *eau de Javel*[5] in the weekly wash tub, which in turn rotted house linen, as indispensable and irreplaceable as the gumboots. Adieu to polished floors as wax and turpentine became unobtainable. No polish within doors, no paint without or within; and so fleas and wood-beetles defied the housewife as did garden pests her husband. The wail from the kitchen went forth

4. A small Basque town.
5. Parazone.

as pots and pans, plates and cups, jugs and cauldrons, went the way of the rest and even earthenware utensils became irreplaceable. Strict gas and electricity rationing, scarcity of coal and the exorbitant price of wood or turf made cooking ever more difficult. Even then we were reduced to soups and stews, for there was no grease or oil for frying. Nowhere more so than in the kitchen, once the pride of the household, did nationwide poverty become more apparent.

In the garden, soon not only chemicals were lacking to spray cabbages or tomatoes, poison slugs and grubs, but to replace a rake, a hoe or spade, to get a yard of chicken-wire or a few feet of wood led to much searching, expense, worry, and, inevitably, frustration. The lack of manures and of composite foods for livestock increased the difficulties when young and old in every family were turning out to work on a vegetable patch. Elderly gentlemen and ladies might be seen shamefacedly collecting treasure deposited by some passing German horse or the milkman's mule, or poking in a neighbour's bin for some oddment of greens that might be acceptable to the family rabbit. Dogs and cats, reduced to bags of bone, led chastened existences. Their skins hung about them like the clothes about their masters and mistresses. Inexorably the grip of fate tightened as *La Grande pitié de France,* unknown since the dim Middle Ages, returned to sweep fair lands and once prosperous homes.

Inevitably, conditions varied from one region to another and were different in occupied and unoccupied territories. Townsfolk suffered more than country people. In general, however, the standard of living throughout France, along with everything else, crashed dramatically after the Armistice. The clearest indication of the national penury can be found in the monthly ration-table which set out, in skeleton form, the pattern of life. Its ten headings made up a national Declaration of Poverty for the world to see. Bereft of trimmings, it meant that the average man or woman was left with a few thin slices of bread per day, one small piece of meat per week, two bottles of wine per month (subsequently increased to four) and a daily pennyweight of fats (oil, grease, butter and cheese often defaulted) with which to condiment any vegetables he or she could find. The sugar ration amounted to two small lumps a day; coffee was a substitute and bread tickets had to be surrendered in return for biscuits or confectionery.

Here follows the full scale with the "extras" that were supposed to make life tolerable and which varied somewhat with the seasons and regions.

I Bread: General ration 275 grammes per day, increased after the harvest of 1943 to 300 grammes and then diminished to 200 grammes after the landing in Normandy in June 1944. Infants 100 grammes; children and old people 200 grammes; growing youths and girls, men engaged in hard labour, 350 grammes.

II Special sweetened flour or meal: 250 grammes per month for infants, children and old people.

III Tapioca and macaroni: Occasionally small quantities were distributed or bread tickets up to 250 grammes were allowed to be exchanged against Tapioca, if and when available.

IV Meat: A variable weekly ration was distributed according to local supplies available, with a supplement of 350 grammes for young men, girls and labourers. It was the duty of the Prefect to fix the ration, which in southwest France averaged about 180 grammes, including bone. (Suet and fat were pared off in the slaughter houses for the collective grease pot.)

V Cheese: 50 grammes per week with a supplement for labourers.

VI Grease and oil, including butter and margarine: 450 grammes per month with supplements of 250 and 450 grammes for workers classed as *travailleurs de force* (miners, stokers, fishermen etc.). Often defaulted.

VII Sugar: General ration 500 grammes per person with supplements of as much again for children and the elderly. Often defaulted.

VIII Rice: Reserved for the young, infants getting 300 grammes, children 200 grammes per month.

IX Chocolate: Infants, children and the elderly 125 grammes; youths of both sexes 250 grammes. Diminished and in many areas defaulted after the loss of Algeria and Morocco in November 1942.

X Coffee: 45 grammes pure grain mixed with 150 grammes ersatz or sometimes chicory. If preferred, 25 grammes tea or 125 grammes tea with ersatz. Only Ersatz was available after November 1942.

What people felt most was the lack of sugar, meat and fats. The bread ration was much less than the average Frenchman was used to, but, even in its dark and gritty form, just sufficient to remain the staff of life. In summer a small supplementary issue of sugar enabled a few pots of jam to be made and, in winter, there were, besides, a few issues of jam and dried fruit. In winter also occasional issues of macaroni and dried vegetables, ranging from 250 grammes to 500 grammes per person per month, were made to counteract the cold. The extra weekly dish of dried beans, lentils or macaroni thus provided, served to remind people of their loss rather than fill any void, for France had always enjoyed a superabundance of such produce. Potatoes disappeared for months at a time; fish became almost unobtainable. Whilst the Government was selling potatoes at Fr3.70 per kilo, the price on the black market was Fr25 and later Fr50. The same was the case with the occasional egg which the *Ravitaillement* was able to distribute at 5 to 10% of the black market price.

In town, vegetables had to be rationed. The ticket issue of greens at Bordeaux amounted to 200 grammes per day. In August 1942, throughout southwest France, grapes were selling at Fr17.50 per kilo, ten times the price of two years previously. And similarly with peaches, pears, carrots and all the rest. A medium-sized cabbage cost Fr10 in 1941, Fr20 in 1942; the prices of sugar and honey, butter and cheese, progressed by leaps and bounds. In fact, commodities outside official issues became priceless. Profiteers demanded and generally got what they wanted. Chicken, rabbit, lobster, foie-gras, salmon, readily available produce in *la France d'antan*,[6] were carefully reserved for the highest bidder. Five thousand francs for a ham. Oh ye shades of *jambonneau de Bayonne*,[7] sweet and succulent, wrapped in thy golden shroud of breadcrumbs, what sayest thou in the valley beyond, of such traffickings!

In full tomato season 1942, when families were filling jars and bottles for winter consumption, the price ranging around 7 francs, an order came fixing the price at 4.50 francs per kilo. The next morning, as if by enchantment, there was not a tomato on the market. The same thing happened with the *Mondarrain*[8] cherries earlier in the year. In former years, for a fortnight or so, Bayonne and the Pays Basque used to enjoy a copious supply of these luscious berries. Now it became a case of queuing, with policemen maintaining order, whenever a stray basket happened to appear on the market. When the Authorities reduced the price from ten to five francs per kilo, presto! all the cherries disappeared. "Let the Bayonnais come and pick them", said the countryfolk.

In the markets and shops, prices of goods were posted up. Uniformed *agents de police* circulated. But right in front of them transactions proceeded at higher tariffs. "Madam will understand that we cannot sell at those prices", murmured the retailer, and, strangely, the public acquiesced. Grocers made large fortunes in a few months and promptly invested the proceeds in property purchases. The names of the villas they purchased were known amongst their customers, victims of extortion as they were. When a catch arrived at the fish market, there would ensue a long squabble between the dealers, each wanting a larger share of the better class of fish. The public queued submissively and waited while the dispute proceeded. As this went on much of the fish disappeared, to be disposed of secretly. The Inspector, after seeing that all livers had been cut out and consigned to the special oil treasury, chalked up the prices. Transactions then began, although, once the Inspector's back was

6. France of old.
7. Cured ham from Bayonne.
8. Mountain of the Basque country.

turned, not always at the prices he had marked. Such was the routine when fish came in from St. Jean de Luz after the greater proportion of the catch had gone to the German-controlled tinning industry.

The *Gazette de Biarritz*,[9] subject like all papers in the Occupied Zone to strict censorship, in an article dated 24 August 1942, summed up the situation as follows:

> "The Price Question: the intentions of the Government are excellent but difficulties unheard of previously now have to be overcome. The Government has declared war against rising prices and the black market although it is evident that, up to the present, price control has been insufficient and measures against the black market remain a dead letter.
>
> Almost all taxed merchandise, whether in market or shop, is sold at counter price. Pretence is made to justify this practice by the supposed scarcity of goods; these goods are reserved for buyers who can and will pay a higher price. Thus a sort of illicit auctioneering takes place unchecked.
>
> As soon as a product is 'taxed' it disappears from official open trade and passes into the black market. Everyone sees it; everyone knows it; everyone speaks of it. Housewives become indignant yet pay the price if they can. Punishment, announced to be terrible as from the skies, like lightning, only strikes an occasional tree in the forest of abuse.
>
> High circles should realise that the food question has become a matter of grave anxiety for the people. It would be well to forestall public indignation".

How different this tame little paragraph to what the *Gazette* would have fulminated in former days; yet how significant.

What was it that thus severed the link between the people and the authorities to the point of creating collusion between victim and

9. Name of local newspaper.

profiteer? What weakened the arm of the law precisely when authority was enthroned as the guiding principle of the Nation and when the public interest appeared to be better served by due exercise of such authority. Indeed, one may ask what it was that breached solidarity amongst Frenchmen and sent one class to prey pitilessly on another in a time of national calamity?

Many factors came in to play to create a new situation. In occupied France, the administration, every cog of which pivoted on the central wheel in Paris, found itself destabilised. A strongly centralised system could only be efficient as long as the centre existed but the division of France into two zones completely undermined such system. Marshal Pétain recognised this inasmuch as he extended the powers of Departmental Prefects, with each province being in greater measure autonomous. This did not suit the Germans who saw to it that the local Authorities remained subservient. And thus the latter, in the eyes of the people, came to be looked down upon as tools of the Germans. The unfortunate Prefects found themselves between the devil and the deep sea. On the one hand it was their duty to uphold the orders of the Kommandanturs while at the same time they were the executive agents receiving instructions from Vichy for stocking and blocking crops and commodities. Also, as often as not, any initiative they might take in the interest of the local populations they were supposed to govern, was promptly curtailed. By the summer of 1942, the livestock population of southwest France had recovered to pre-war levels. This fact, announced in the local press together with the proposal of the prefectural authority, in accordance with its attributions, to increase somewhat the meagre meat ration, caused rejoicing; short-lived, however, for instead of an increase, heavier German requisitions followed.

Thus, as soon as any effort, collective or individual, produced results, the one thought of the producer was to conceal it from the Germans and French Authorities alike and to sell as much of it as possible on personal account. Thus the black market became a triangular battle between the Germans, intent on requisitioning everything down to the grain for sowing, the French Authorities, burdened with the duty of securing enough food to maintain the standard of rationing they'd set up, and the farmer or individual intent on saving all he could both from the Germans and the *Ravitaillement* and taking a nice profit on the way. The common belief that, if the Government got the goods, the Germans would procure them in the long run, made the public tolerant of profiteers and traffickers. On the other hand, the German Authorities (as distinct from the soldiers who became patrons of the black market) were exasperated by both the extent of the 'fraud' and the failure of the food controllers to assert themselves, to the point of believing that the people and Police were conniving against them, which, of course, to a certain extent was true.

Thus, by a strange irony the *marché noir* that preyed upon them and caused the cost of living constantly to rise, found, if not justification, at least toleration in the eyes of the people. The incompetence and even dishonesty of some of the Inspectors and Commissioners sent down to supervise the collection and distribution of supplies contributed to further undermining the scant confidence people had in the government. This sense of disgust was only to be expected when they could see potatoes, of which they were deprived, being stocked and allowed to rot, or blocked beans became worm-eaten, and wine turning sour. This criminal waste, which even the Germans could not prevent, went unpunished. Locally, there was the great cod fish scandal in Bayonne and the separate story, published in detail in the Press, of the Inspector who sold saccharine clandestinely to certain dealers at a fantastic price, only then to confiscate it from them "*au nom de la loi*".

Some adventurers tried to double-cross the Germans only generally to rue it, for the latter were in a privileged position to defend themselves. There were also Germans who, with French accomplices, dabbled in the French markets, as the records of the Bayonne law courts reveal.

These moral miseries added to the general distress for they were the continuous subject of comment wherever one happened to be and whatever one was doing. In the sickly atmosphere of doubt and suspicion these miseries took on more importance than was warranted. "*Où allons nous*" was the anguished cry often heard in a society which, feeling itself defenceless, lay seemingly at the mercy of events.

Chapter 6

Aftermath of Defeat

During the long miserable years following the Armistice, Frenchmen in all walks of life, while wrestling with the hardship of occupation, the poisons of propaganda and the preoccupations of everyday life, had ample time to reflect on the causes that had reduced France to such miserable straits. Unlike the Gaullists abroad, who preserved their liberty and with it their self-respect as well as faith in the future of the Third Republic, the marooned inhabitants of Metropolitan France, reduced to servitude, took a despondent view and were ready to burn the gods they had once adored. In the gloom of humiliation, a spate of books appeared pouring vitriol on the régime which had been sacrificed in the Casino at Vichy. This culminated in a monumental outpouring of spite, hatred and turpitude in a publication which, although originally priced at 65 francs in 1942, was selling two years later for between four and five thousand francs. Only morbid factors can account for such a phenomenal success. Indifferently printed on poor paper, and without any special pretentions to literary style, *Les Décombres*[10] serves to illustrate the depth of recrimination into which the French population had plunged and the burning desire for a collective scapegoat on which to discharge individual qualms of conscience.

Even those who had least sympathy with defeatist doctrines were ready to round on Marianne and take her as a Turk's head on which to unload the accumulated bitterness of several generations, forgetting that she could only be what they themselves had made her.

Ah! *La pourriture de la politique!*[11] How Frenchmen suddenly loathed the insincerities about which they had formerly laughed, the intrigues

10. "The ruins".
11. The rottenness of politics.

they had countenanced and even practised. "I hate the lies that have done such harm", exclaimed Marshal Pétain, and his *cri de coeur* echoed from the Ardennes to the Pyrenees. They had led to the collapse of an imposing administrative machine and of the army, last hope of the Nation, succumbing with everything else. History repeats itself: Marshal Lefebvre's existing gaiter buttons, Pierre Cot's non-existent aeroplanes, the former a symbol of 1870, the latter of 1939, both leading to the stark reality of disaster.

Viewed through the sad eyes of 1940, public life under the Third Republic appeared indeed to have sunk to the lowest level: democracy become a sordid farce, the sovereignty of the Nation a fiction, liberty non-existent, equality a pretence, fraternity at a minimum. The more French men and women reflected, the clearer the picture seemed to emerge, however unpalatable to their patriotism. Poor Marianne – how she had been betrayed! What right had she to wear the Phrygian cap any longer? What had become of the enduring principles of 1789? Universal suffrage indeed, with only 28% of the Nation allowed to vote and of the voters only a minority represented in Parliament. With 10% of the Nation making the laws for the rest, what becomes of national sovereignty, of liberty? Equality indeed, with no proportional representation for minorities; women asked to pay taxes but refused the right to vote and, in this respect, placed on a par with criminals and lunatics; direct taxation for only 7% of the population; the right to teach and the right of association refused to the Religious, declared a class of pariahs; the political sphere infringing on the judiciary; and favouritism rampant in all branches of public life! Fraternity indeed! Equally, the Declaration of the Rights of Man remained unrecognised in a Constitution depriving individuals all recourse against oppression and also of all initiatives to propose or ratify legislation. Under such a régime, lagging far behind other modern democracies, a citizen became, as Louis Veuillot, a member of the Right, put it: "a Mr I-don't-know-what by a decree of a Mr I-don't-know-who" or as Georges Clemenceau, a member of the Left, averred "reduced to content himself like the Gods of Homer with the smoke of sacrifice".

Many warnings over many years had remained unheeded while men of the Left appeared as ready as those of the Right to wield power by Decree, content to pay lip service to democracy, poisoning it finally in the minds of men of goodwill. The worst example had been that of Léon Blum and the Front Populaire in 1936 when conditions became little less than chaotic and the spectre of Civil War loomed, clouding perception of the impending great European tragedy.

It now became clear how the rot at home had prevented any continuity of foreign policy, so that France's position weakened from year to year. Incoherent in the extreme, the socialist and communist unions both clamoured against militarism and sabotaged military preparations, while insisting on bellicose policies and remaining defiant towards Germany, Italy and Franco's Spain. Unsurprisingly, French fascists refused to "die for Danzig". National issues became shrouded by party views. Frenchmen in all camps drifted under the influence of warring ideologies to the point where the Nation was not only losing faith in its leaders but also in itself.

It was at this juncture, torn by factions, that France was propelled into war by the rush of world events. A house divided was bound to fall. In that cursed autumn of 1939 no *union sacrée* was possible, unlike 1914. Parliament was not even consulted, so little store did the leaders of the day set on what should have been the backbone of the régime. No wonder the people lost confidence in their political class. Eight months of *la drôle de guerre* culminated in the shame and misery of the *sauve qui peut*[12] of June 1940. The supreme test for nations had caught France materially and morally unprepared. It was while recalling all this, stewing as it were in the miseries of defeat, that Frenchmen passed their unhappiest hours.

After the Armistice, there France lay to be mercilessly plundered and exploited by a pitiless enemy. Not only by the enemy, alas! With ruin and disaster came many opportunities for the unscrupulous and greedy, for tricksters and intriguers, so clever at picking a living

12. Every man for himself.

or amassing a fortune by any means available. They had lived by deceiving the Republic and would continue to live – they hoped – by deceiving the Germans. Duplicity has its price but this didn't bother them. As it had been, so it would be – all at the expense of the Nation. *Primum vivere* was their moto, so "collaboration" was welcome for the opportunities it brought. Thus there were Germans being entertained by Frenchmen who, at a later hour, listened to the BBC and professed ardent Gaullist sentiments.

Their only excuse was that the Germans were everywhere and controlled all raw materials; had a stranglehold on industry and trade; were in a position either to plunder or protect industry and agriculture; and held the reins of employment. The Germans paid generously, though still with French francs, of course.

Patriots who would have no dealings with the Germans paid the penalty of poverty and were left to wrestle with all types of difficulties. The bitterness felt at seeing the advantages secured by "collaborators" increased the divisions among Frenchmen. Nonetheless, any fortunes made did not induce profiteers to waste much love on the Occupiers. German officers claimed their share of profits and when nefarious dealings became too scandalously obvious it was the Frenchmen who ended up in prison. Trafficking in confiscated Jewish property was one of the ugliest features of this get-rich-quick period.

This whole sordid story served to revolt the broad mass of the French against the Occupier. It also served an economic purpose and helped keep France going, though ruinously. The black market became by far the biggest business in the country. Countless thousands found both means of livelihood and sustenance therein.

There were of course those who collaborated in all good faith. They did so for various motives. Some because they were out-and-out pacifists and placed more faith in spiritual than material force and believed in the French power to "humanise the inhuman". They visualised France throughout this period of submission as continuing to assert her civilising influence by dint of docility, perseverance and attachment to the ways of peace, the wiles of sentiment, finally to triumph through

Germany's conversion. Others, on the contrary, collaborated because they believed in Prussian military superiority and saw its consecration in the crushing defeat inflicted on France. This group joined with admirers of German efficiency and especially of national-socialism as a doctrine for eliminating class strife in a desire to see France become the principal partner in a new European order under German hegemony. France's defeat being real and undeniable, had it not become a high French interest to compound with the enemy and seek reconciliation, even to the extent of a reversal of alliances? Hitler seemed ready to pose as a disciple of Frederick II and there were modern Voltaires ready to act as intermediaries.

Alongside these committed collaborationists were others who, while jibbing at an alliance with Germany and declaring war on England, were anxious to save France from becoming a battleground. Unhappy with Great Britain for not having brought sufficiently strong initial aid to the coalition, they lost faith in, though not altogether sympathy with the British cause. These good people knew England so little that they believed she would not dare invade France to get at Germany if France showed her teeth. They knew Germany so little that they believed France could strike a bargain with Hitler enabling France to be mistress in her own house and to rearm on the strength of a solely defensive Alliance.

Then there was the ever-present Bolshevist menace looming above the war clouds. The genuine fear of Communism, innate in the most conservative bourgeoisie in Europe, brought many recruits ready to gather behind the German barrier to the East. If indeed the greater number of young Frenchmen were intent on escaping by dangerous routes to the camp of the Allies, others, no less inspired by generous sentiments of sacrifice, joined the anti-Bolshevist Legion in the frozen wastes of Russia. Disgust at seeing Mr Churchill, so long an energetic adversary of the Soviets, become a panegyrist of Stalin and also apparently ready to sacrifice Poland and Yugoslavia to Bolshevism, turned many Frenchmen's thoughts, if not their hearts, from London towards Berlin.

There were yet other Frenchmen obsessed exclusively with internal politics. Which was the way out for the new *État Français*? Monarchy and Catholicism having been politically abolished in France there was no basis for foundation on either of these traditions. But the lost traditions might arise again if the new Government could succeed in creating favourable conditions by re-establishing national unity around a legitimate authority, effectively the same issue as at the time of the Wars of Religion. As in 1552, the French State in 1944 must be rescued from the parties and the Nation from virtual civil war.

Others again favoured attempting to draw Latin Europe into collaboration with Germany so as to utilise Spain and Portugal (respectively non-belligerent and neutral) as counterweights in the establishment of a new Continental order. They hoped that Germany would not take pure revenge for Iéna but would realise, by virtue of what followed Iéna, that it is impossible to suppress a Nation of forty million souls and that in the long run it is less profitable to oppress than to collaborate. They also hoped that genuine collaboration would lead eventually, not only to reconciliation with Germany, but also with Italy, in an enlarged sphere of European reorganisation.

Such were some of the considerations, plans, thoughts, doubts and even hopes which assailed Frenchmen in the months following the collapse, whilst the situation was to a great extent fluid and the flood of possibilities let loose by France's fall from high position as a Great Power still existed in the period before major events settled matters.

All these cogitations, however, from wherever they came, ran up eventually against the same stone wall – the hard fact that the war continued. Moreover, as months and years passed, the sphere of conflict, instead of remaining circumscribed to Germany versus England, spread both East and West until it finally encompassed the Globe. The possibility of defeat for Great Britain, which might have brought an early 'peace', disappeared and the scope of the conflict was greatly magnified.

While all these events proceeded, groups and parties were forming, taking up position and becoming rooted in prejudice, the plant that grows so rapidly when wishes evolve into beliefs in an atmosphere of depression and privation.

German propaganda was quick to get to work and vested interests took a share in exploiting dreams, encouraging delusions and warping interpretation. Paris became the headquarters of a great drive to convert Frenchmen to Germanophilia. The immense resources of the capital for journalism, printing and publication, music and art, were cleverly utilised. Craftsmen and artisans as well as artists, writers and intellectuals, all somehow had to live. One of the reasons the Germans tried so hard to convince Marshal Pétain to transfer the seat of Government from Vichy to Paris was because of the opportunities it would bring them to break down barriers and complete the subjugation of the French Press. So long as the bitter war of words continued between Paris and Vichy, the Germans felt that Vichy would hold the stage. But if there were only one bell and one sound!

As it was they soon had a powerful Press at work, enjoying advantages and privileges of paper supply. They found tame writers who made the French section of the *Pariser Zeitung* quite readable. In *La Gerbe*,[13] Alphonse de Chateaubriant produced a news organ preaching fascist doctrines. With *Révolution Nationale* they usurped the subtitle of the Vichy Régime and endeavoured to dictate its rules of conduct. In *Je Suis Partout*[14] they roped in a clique of anglophobe journalists who had already done their best to poison Franco-British relations in the years preceding the war. *Combats, Temps Nouveaux,*[15] *Germinal* and many others made up a confusing kaleidoscope.

Assailed from every direction, Frenchmen nevertheless remained impenetrable and kept their own counsel. They bought the German papers because a Frenchmen must have something to read and his wife something with which to light the fire. Then there were the pictures of *Signal*; but, alas, *Signal* proved all but incombustible! *Panorama* was a welcome exception, an oasis in a desert of deceit. A weekly, well

13. The Sheaf.
14. I am everywhere.
15. New Times.

printed and illustrated on good paper, eschewing politics altogether, it fulfilled its purpose of giving some account of what was happening in the world of art and letters while the war went on.

Flamboyant posters covered the walls all over France. One remembers some of them more for their artistic merit rather than for what they represented. Against a rising sun labelled 1941 – how hopeful were the Germans then! – a beautiful French girl, appropriately bare-footed, is planting a lowly shrub. A man, wearing a beret, with business-like rolled up sleeves, who was digging the hole, has arisen and is facing three wolves labelled Free masonry, Jewry and de Gaulle. Instead of going for the wolves with his spade, the man makes a gesture of shaking them off, shouting "Leave us alone". In the circumstances, onlookers were left to guess whom the tree was being planted for.

Joan of Arc, Napoleon, Mers-el-Kébir, the bombing of French towns, and Churchill incongruously depicted in a tin hat and with an enormous cigar or as a multi-tentacled octopus, all figured time and again. The Germans seemed to lack imagination, so often did the same subjects recur. A Special Collection was dedicated to recruiting labour for Germany. These were scarcely more subtle: "At last we are happy", explains a little girl to her mother, "Papa is working in Germany." Despite the cheery circumstances depicted – bread and jam, clean overalls, spotless cottage and workshop – they communicated a deep and sad perversion of the truth. Then there was the poster into which the designer, perhaps a starving but ingenious Gaullist, contrived to infuse a double-meaning: a dejected French soldier in torn uniform and battered helmet carries on bent shoulders a huge Cross, supposed to represent the burden of English oppression. Everybody, however, understood what the Cross really represented, as the word "Hitler", scrawled in a child's handwriting on the Cross, in one case showed.

French people drew and painted these posters and earned a living in doing so. They also gazed at them. Did they take them to heart? For one thing, the posters never lasted long; perhaps the paste was ersatz or watered; and the stripping from the walls was certainly helped along by old and young alike. They were also often pasted in series of four, whereupon it was easy, after nightfall, for a confederate of objectors to paint a large numeral on each of them (one, nine, one, eight) so that at a little distance they appeared to advertise some event in connection with 1918. The posters were everywhere, just as German literature overflowed from the *Buchshandlung* set up in all towns into every newspaper kiosk. There was an old lady at Tarbes,[16] enthroned in the middle of the railway hall, who had ideas of her own about displaying her merchandise to advantage. *Signal* had published cover pictures of Churchill and Roosevelt, full-sized if rather villainous images. Around this she had arranged all the other papers in radiating lines so that the heads of the British Premier and American President were at the centre of a sort of constellation over which she herself presided, grim or smiling according to whether the approaching customer was German or French. No one entering or leaving the busy station could miss the show.

A few days before Rome was liberated, posters appeared showing a map of Italy with two snails creeping up it, labelled "British and American Armies". A calculation based on the rate of progress made over previous months had indicated that Rome was out of reach for a very long time. That poster remained unmolested much longer than the others.

Why, one wonders, didn't the Germans take it down? They were quick enough in some things: When the V campaign began, on the walls of German billets and even on their motor cars, they took on the job themselves, covering tunics, doors, cars and horses with Vs enshrined in laurel wreaths, thus effectively swamping the clandestine effort. How this grew and took another, more serious shape, is another story: The story of *La Résistance*.

16. Town near the Pyrenees.

Chapter 7
La Résistance

The development of the Resistance was a case of spontaneous political evolution. In its early stages, the Resistance owed nothing to anyone and was simply the result of each Frenchman thinking for himself – an entirely free decision. Cut off from the Free French abroad, instinctively distrusting Vichy and its "kollaboration", unable to communicate thoughts openly to his peers over the café table, with freedom gone and nothing to drink, what could Jean Français do but think it all through for himself. He wasn't alone, however, because thousands were going through the same process of deep reflection as to the current state of France and what was to be done about it. Each one finally drew from the deep well of national character, far below the surface, the same draught of vivifying waters. The result was something special, taking some time and for which these patriots probed deeply into their inner selves. The spring, once tapped, flowed initially with the secrecy of welling waters, to be merged subsequently in the relentlessness of a tide.

Once committed, every concerned individual had the very real problem of how to give expression to their innermost thoughts, an immensely complicated process and fraught with far-from-imaginary perils. In the régime of make-believe that was Pétain's *État Français,* it was imperative to hide one's thoughts until sure of one's interlocutor, a tortuous process and one in which so many paid for any indiscretion with imprisonment or worse.

Many months passed before patriots began to communicate, first in groups, then between groups, until finally, greatly aided by the changed international situation, it became possible to evolve a common scheme of action. In the early stages, individuals could do little but act negatively, each in his own sphere and according to his circumstances. Nevertheless, however minor, such passive resistance could be astonishingly effective and was, moreover, contagious.

One recalls a resolute old lady who possessed a large Villa. She had brought up a family but sons and daughters were married and she remained alone with the servants – comfortable rooms, solid old furniture, an ideal billet for German Officers, or at least so they thought until they got there. They had ordered her out and gave her three days' notice. When she left she took everything with her, from garret to cellar. Presses built into walls were torn out and all electric fittings, lamps and switches were removed. She even took the door handles. She then settled herself, somewhat uncomfortably, in a farmhouse within view and earshot of her dismantled home. The Germans found it uninviting and for nearly a year the big house remained unoccupied. Finally, it was turned into a dressing station in connection with an adjacent airfield. The airfield was bombed and great damage was done all around. Providentially, neither the old lady nor her cow was hit. The Germans rendered one service: at her request they removed a dud bomb from the farm. Had it exploded whilst they did so, no doubt she would have been quite content. Such was the Resistance.

Across the country, the above trivial instance could be multiplied a thousandfold. Grains of sand mount up.

In contrast to individual resistance is the collective case of the SNCF, the National Railways of France. The *cheminots*, as railwaymen are called, had to run a service which would allow people to continue with normal life under the occupation. Their's was also the sorry task of carrying away to Germany, for the Germans, the vast loot seized in France, as well as the products of industry. In every station of any size a German Railway Transport Officer was posted. Half the coaches on every train were reserved for the Army of Occupation. Expresses ran from Hendaye to Berlin. There was no avoiding the servitude though so many cases of sabotage occurred that the Germans were obliged to reinforce the RTOs with squads of German railwaymen. When the Resistance began blowing up railway tracks, or more effectively still, blowing down the standards carrying powerlines over the long stretches of electrified track existing in France, a grand game of battledore and shuttlecock ensued. When communications were cut on the Bordeaux line, for instance, the goods stream towards Germany would be switched via Toulouse. If the Pyrenean mainline then got blocked, the traffic would have to return via Bordeaux, reopened once more only to be cut again. In this manner, whole trainloads of precious olive oil remained in France and the stocks of Spanish mineral ores on the quays of Bayonne overflowed into the broad avenues along the Adour river.

When the RAF began systematic bombing of the rail network, French engine-drivers met death on the footboard. When the planes appeared they brought their trains to a halt – if not killed before they could do so – and took their chance. They didn't shirk their duty. Rightly, the Government subsequently rewarded their conduct, for their sacrifice represented the ultimate service to the Nation. Here is the Order of the Nation citation concerning one Albert Victor Joseph Michel, killed on 6 February 1943: "Engine-driver, fourteen times attacked, twice wounded. Gave a fine example of professional courage by continuing on duty in exposed districts until fatally wounded at his post." Such men as Michel, though obliged to serve the Germans, were no less serving France. Such was the tragic fate of many Frenchmen. They also helped many parachutists and airmen who'd been shot down to escape. And when the long-awaited time came, the *cheminots* of the Resistance were ready to act directly in support of the Allied landings.

The Resistance could never have spread as it did without the support it received everywhere. It became the greatest national conspiracy that ever existed. Its agents cleaned the boots of German officers in hotels and also sat at table with Marshal Pétain and Laval. All such representatives of officialdom were spied on for information that might be put to use for the Cause. The result was a secret organisation that, for one thing, enabled Allied agents to travel from one end of France to the other. A disabled airman was safe provided it was a Frenchman and not a German who found him.

One day, in the remote corner of southwest France to which we were exiled by the Germans, three men passed along the road. Two were American airmen speaking not a word of French who would become prisoners of war if found. The third, their guide, if discovered with them, would be doomed. They had cycled down from the Loire region where clothes and bicycles – and how rare and precious had bicycles become by 1943 – were given to them to speed them on their way; all at immense risk and because they were Allied soldiers. It may have seemed to the men and women who gave up their bicycles that the airmen had but one chance in a thousand to reach the frontier but, just to enable them to get that chance, they handed over their precious items whilst also risking arrest as accomplices. All along those hundreds of miles they had been passed from place to place and agent to agent. Finally they were within site of the frontier and could see the peaks through which they would pass if all went well.

If all went well, indeed. They did not know what had befallen three comrades of theirs at Lendresse,[17] a little village on the Gave,[18] a bare mile from where they were now passing. Those three lads, met at the railway station of Lacq by Truber, the engineer at the local electric transformer station, and taken to his house, were dazzled by the beauty of the Pyrenean foothills in Spring. They sunbathed and dallied by the Gave-side. Truber's wife and daughter made life very pleasant for them. Three weeks later the Gestapo appeared and carried off Truber and the three truants. Sometime after this, Truber's wedding ring was sent back to his wife. Long afterwards, when Pau was liberated, a message was found scribbled in pencil on the walls of a Gestapo prison, signed Truber of Lacq: succour my wife and family. The three Americans were freed when the Maquisards[19] captured Toulouse and the prison camps nearby.

The history of the Resistance will occupy historians for many years to come. It can be said with some confidence that the tale they reveal will equal in heroism the open fights waged by the Free French. The latter had their banner with the proud Cross of Lorraine fluttering

17. Village near Pau.
18. Fast-flowing river.
19. Men of the Resistance, from "maquis" in its original sense, a scrub land in Corsica.

to the breezes of heaven in the four corners of the world but the men and women of the Resistance had no flag. The Tricolour was banned, banished everywhere but from their hearts. They lived only to serve it, despite it being soiled by the actions of Vichy. In between the fighting, the Free French were free, free in a hundred ways not open to the harried French people who, besides their worries, had to live surrounded by Germans at every corner, obliged to constant dissimulation and secrecy, a strain that never let up night or day. For them there was no relaxation, none except for the secret sessions listening to the hooded wireless sets. How French life hung throughout those years on the BBC! But that is another story.

During the long formation period of the Resistance, only a Frenchman's indomitable will enabled him to continue, completely dependent on himself as he was. He trusted no one whilst nonetheless sensing dimly that he could trust most other Frenchmen to feel as he did. And so it turned out because otherwise there could be no resistance.

Little by little groups were formed around the bolder and more assertive characters. They became the leaders, the ones most useful to the enemy and therefore those whose identity had to remain hidden at all costs. Simple pseudonyms were used, some of which were ultimately to achieve local fame: Achille, Georges, Aristide of the Pyrenees, Leon of the Landes, even the frivolous but stout Fri-Fri. These local movements, however small and fragile, provided their military and civilian "services" and generally produced a clandestine news sheet, normally with a clarion title such as *Combat, Libération, or Franc-Tireur.*

The movements became amalgamated into the MUR, "*Mouvements Unis de la Résistance*". Later, when political associations such as the Communist *Front National* claimed a share in the Resistance, the MUR became the MLN "*Mouvement de la Libération Nationale*", and finally the National Council of Liberation was formed, the central body that had representatives in Algiers.

Nonetheless, the basis and strength of the entire movement depended on local men and local action. This was normal, not only because of the need for effective communication with the speed required for successful combined military action between irregulars, but also because knowledge of the countryside and the sympathy of the country people were essential to success. A *Maquisard* who could speak the local *patois* was doubly fortunate.

This perhaps explains the set-back in Savoy when Alphonso, with his mixed band of Czechs, Poles, and Spaniards, took to the fields and surroundings where they were unknown.

Villagers were ready to take risks for the local *Maquis* while remaining suspicious of intruding foreign bands. Getting it wrong would produce fatal results. In the Dordogne, a butcher who had supplied meat to the *Maquisards* was shot by the Germans. They brought the corpse to his house, flung it through one of the windows and set the place on fire. Elsewhere whole villages[20] were destroyed after the inhabitants had been executed *en masse.* No aid to the *Maquisards* was considered too small for it not to be considered criminal. At Bagnères in the Pyrenees a shoemaker who sold them sandals and a doctor who had attended their sick were punished severely. Such savageness could have but one effect – to kill all prospect of collaboration and immensely fortify the Resistance.

The story of the *Maquis* is essentially one of local action until, towards the end, the parachuting of Allied officers and the increasing abundance of arms and war material enabled action to be militarily co-ordinated on a wider scale.

When the Germans consented by the terms of the Armistice to the French people being administered by French officials they made a great mistake. It had allowed the people to retain a separate sense of identity and forfeited the only chance of coercing them. Moreover, the Unoccupied Zone of the *État Français,* despite the German Commissions and policy of collaboration, became the real centre of the Resistance, its great Keep, whence much of the planning was carried out and whence the vast majority of the escapes to the ranks

20. Oradour (alas, famous).

of the Allies were effected. To cross the demarcation line was the first stage to obtaining freedom.

The *Deuxième Bureau*, the Intelligence Branch of what was left of the Army, mostly co-operated with the Resistance, either directly or through confederates. Even after the Germans invaded the Vichy Zone, sensational escapes such as those of Generals Giraud and Delattre de Tassigny continued to happen. In the Police, among prison officials and in all branches of the Administration, helpers were always to be found. The Navy was less fertile ground – Mers el Kébir and Dakar rankled. When Admiral Darlan turned his coat for the second time, he failed to take the Toulon Fleet to Africa with him. Those grand modern ships perished miserably but they were never surrendered to the Germans. In giving his order for the sinking, Marshal Pétain remained faithful to French commitments to Great Britain concerning the Navy, come what might.

The Marshal's inclination was always to take Frenchmen as he found them. Some of his closest associates were useful members of the Resistance. There can be no doubt about the services they rendered. When Laval tried to 'purify' the Vichy Administration, the first and most lasting effect of his efforts was to drive more adherents into the Resistance camp. A large and valuable contingent passed across when the French Army of 100,000 men, permitted under the Armistice, was dissolved in November 1942. Knowing that their ultimate end would be internment in Germany, officers and men went underground in any way they could. Content to serve under the Marshal's flag, so long as it kept the members of the Army together in France, in the hope perhaps of eventually being able to turn even the poor weapons they possessed against the hated enemy, officers and men were ready to transfer to the Resistance when the crisis came. Such also was the case with the *Chantiers de la Jeunesse*[21] which the Marshal had established under General de la Porte du Theil. These also mostly passed to the

21. Youth camps.

Resistance, principal ally in France of *La Dissidence*, as the Pétainists referred to the Gaullists.

It seems beyond doubt that the Resistance owes much to the Pétain régime whose advent produced the initial shock that startled the French spirit into resistance. Disaster had reached unfathomable depths when a Marshal of France surrendered. The existence of an *État Français*, however wing-clipped, was certainly more favourable for the workings of a secret network than would have been a régime of German occupation and administration, impervious to penetration or subversion. Apart from the Marshal, who remained an endeared and respected figure to many Frenchmen to the end, even a Laval was preferable in office to a Gauleiter. His efforts, injurious as they were, remained far less effective and repressive than would have been the case with a German. It took a full three years before Laval could begin to organise Darnand's Militia. All so much time gained for the Resistance to establish itself and gain strength.

The hatred concentrated against the Militia, as great if not greater than that felt for the Germans, gives the measure of the depth of patriotic fervour that animated the Resistance. Such hatred between Frenchmen is rare in history. When Militia and Gendarmes were sent against them, the *Maquisards* knew well that the latter would shoot high or wide, but the Militia were set on a par with the Germans as ferocious and despicable. They were, in their way, fanatics.

At last the great day dawned when the Germans began their long retreat from the Pyrenees. On their harassed march across Béarn, they passed many crosses bedecked with flowers and marking sites where men of the Resistance had fallen; the four crosses near Simacourbe where as many *Maquisard*s perished bravely, each stepping into the place of a fallen comrade to man a machine gun protecting a nearby parachute-drop; the isolated grave of a lonely sniper near Biron, and how many, many others! But all were bright with summer flowers laid lovingly on the double Crosses of Lorraine.

This was the first expression of public sentiment at the Liberation – gratitude to the dead and thankfulness for the living. The wide rejoicing that broke out as the last German disappeared was tempered by these funereal scenes. Everywhere the first public demonstration was to place wreaths at the *Monuments aux Morts pour la Patrie.*[22] Sometimes, as at Dax, there were British dead alongside French comrades. Captain Mellow, an Officer belonging to a Scottish Regiment, killed in action nearby, was given a great funeral at the Cathedral. The whole town attended and touching homage was paid to the dead Officer.

At Orthez and all along the road to Pau, villagers and school children with flowers assembled to greet the 'Americans', for somehow the people could not believe that Allied troops were not operating with the irregular bands of the *Maquis.* The only 'Americans' who appeared, however, were a triumphant band of *Maquisards* freshly armed with what had arrived in a considerable parachute-drop the night before and who were hot-foot on the track of the retreating Germans ten miles beyond Orthez. This band had pinned on their sleeves the small American flags parachuted with the rifles and munitions. They made a brief apparition on the square at Orthez where the assembled crowds cheered America and the Allies throughout the afternoon.

A couple of days later I set out by train for Biarritz to see what had become of my home during our fifteen months of exile. There was a wait at Puyoo Junction for over an hour. The junction station was no longer the dreary place it had become under the Occupation. Chairs and tables had been set out under nearby sycamores and wine was flowing instead of the ersatz Bovril made with burnt onion that had so long been the only beverage procurable in the wayside restaurant. Along the platform, in and out of the canteen, travellers swarmed everywhere. On one of the shunting tracks stood a long goods train captured from the Germans. It was composed of half a dozen open trucks. A man of the *Maquis*, clad in ski-trousers and boots, rolled-up shirt sleeves and open collar, stood proudly on guard over the train. An FFI armband with the Croix de Lorraine, a revolver and belt with

22. War Memorials.

ammunition pouches, were his only equipment. In the waiting passenger train someone began to play an accordion.

Sur le pont d'Avignon
On y danse On y danse
Sur le pont d'Avignon
On y danse tous en rond

The simple tune known the world over, even before the BBC adopted it as the call note for one of its services, began to catch on. Inviting and insistent, somehow it responded as nothing else could to the humour of the crowd, one of joyful *insouciance*,[23] after years of constraint. The *Maquisard* on guard, stiff to attention up to then, relaxed. His feet began to twitch and soon, rifle in hand, he was performing a sort of jig. Someone held out a skin of wine to him from a coach window. Leaving his post, he stepped across the tracks, had a good swig and then performed a *pas seul* back to his duty.

People began whistling, others humming the tune. Passengers dance-shuffled along the platform irrespective of age, dangling bundles and bags. Girls and boys hopped, skipped and bounded in abandon. Children took up the chorus. The Station Master was not above cutting a caper. The scene became a wild medley. Only the Gendarme looked on gravely, arms folded over his belt. He was above such temptations.

Then came the climax after which everyone suddenly stopped and looked about rather sheepishly while peals of mirthful laughter made the iron roof of the station ring. Such was the atmosphere of *La Libération* several days after the fact. French people hardly knew whether they stood on their head or their heels those days, almost hysterical was their joy. It seemed hardly possible, after the prolonged nightmare of four interminable years, that the hated Boche had disappeared, as it were, overnight.

23. Carefree feeling.

Chapter 8
Biarritz

March 1943, March 1944, August 1944

In 1943 an early Spring followed a mild winter, the more welcome as the two previous winters had been bitter and, in any case, wood was scarce. People were paying 500 francs a *stère*,[24] whereas it used to be seven! Bright sun lit up the rocky coast while fleeting clouds chased each other merrily across the blue sky, to be speared and caught on some jagged peak. The play of sunlight and cloud gave mobility to the landscape.

So little does nature wreck man or his works, do he his damndest. And forsooth the invader was doing his utmost to ruin the Côte d'Argent, gem of the Atlantic seaboard. New branch railway lines with their cuttings and embankments appeared; hideous blockhouses and strong points ruined the fair coastal scenery above Hendaye. Socoa and Sainte Barbe, the two promontories closing the perfect curve of St. Jean de Luz bay, were slashed and scarred, resembling rubbish-heaps. Tunnels dug into the cliffs under the Côte des Basques spewed greasy slag, polluting the golden strand. Monstrous excavations disfigured the Atalaye and the grass expanse in front of the Hotel du Palais, swallowing up tons of cement, rubble and steel. Rusty *chevaux de frise* cluttered up every exit from the beach; barbed wire defiled the Rocher de la Vierge and the cliffs; the white lighthouse was painted black; big hotels and villas had been gutted and turned into forts; streets, gardens and fields torn up to bury electric power and telephone lines leading to the batteries; and machine-gun nests lay in every direction. Trim streets and squares had become shambles of shovelled earth and

24. Stère equals 1 cubic metre.

scattered stone. Big hotels had been ruined by use as barracks and when one became dirty and dilapidated, the Germans moved onto another. Owners of de-requisitioned buildings found them stripped of metal fittings, piping, bath taps, door handles. Several villas had been turned into brothels, others into prisons. No one living along the coast could be sure of tenure; notice to quit within three days was the fate of many a proud owner of a privileged coastal property. The pinewoods at Chiberta,[25] the Golf Club and racecourse with their large adjacent villas, were a vast devastated area populated with batteries and strong points and littered with broken crockery and furniture. House looting was rife, with civilian thieves joining in.

From the coast and the town clustering round the disused little harbour, the devastation spread inland. The fine old estate of Parme, ancient oaks and all, was levelled to enlarge the adjoining airfield. The red coats of the hunt would never meet there again. Spiteful destruction of the monuments to Empress Eugenie, Queen Victoria and King Edward VII endeavoured to efface the trace of a gracious past. Queen Nathalie, the Crown Prince of Serbia and Russian Grand Dukes were but a memory. The Russian Church was there, its dome freshly painted blue, with the ministering Pope, after his arrest, serving the Germans as interpreter, though without cutting his long straight hair nor doffing his flowing robe, a strangely pathetic figure befitting the place of outcasts Biarritz had become.

Successive evacuation orders had driven away most of the residents. Under threat of invasion, German headquarters had been withdrawn from the seafront to Anglet and Bayonne. Walkers were restricted to the Grande Plage and the road round by the aquarium to the Port Vieux. Bathers had to jostle with the Germans for the patch of beach opposite the Casino.

Gone were the proud divisions which had arrived, flushed with victory, to sprawl in the luxurious quarters provided by the Grand Hotels along the sunny beaches. These fine fellows lay dead on eastern

25. Pine forest near Biarritz.

battlefields; they would never return to see the rich and prosperous Biarritz they had marched into, now bedraggled and degraded. *Gott in Himmel!* what would they have thought of these warriors of the Reich 1943 marching down the hill past the old British Club, at their head a hollow-chested, spindle-legged Hauptmann labouring in the contortions of the goose-step, spectacles strapped to nose and behind him a troop of stiff-jointed clodhoppers and weak-kneed clerks. Every second man wore glasses and all, except the hoary peasants, staggered under the weight of their equipment. They sang to show how carefree the German warrior felt. But gone was the full-chested chant of the fit and strong. The chorus of gruff and quavering voices essayed a tune the older men might have heard floating across from British trenches in Flanders or Picardy, a tune popular when the British Army had its back to the wall in 1917–18, yet which, by some whim of destiny, the German Army had adopted during the triumphant days of 1939–40. As "Pack up your troubles in your old kit bag" reverberated along the Biarritz streets one wondered how long it would be before it rang out in the vernacular. Meanwhile the Ersatz would do, sung by those miserable combings of the medical board, for it evoked a brave memory and perchance carried an omen.

The wretched troop marched downhill. One watched them a couple of hours later as they toiled up and you would understand at once the level to which the German Army of Occupation had fallen and feel the raging impotence of the French, guarded and oppressed by such.

The summer, a long succession of sunny weeks, dragged by. There were no holiday crowds to enjoy the glorious, golden hours. Prohibition to bathe in the sea, other than with the Germans, accentuated the feeling among the French that they were being tracked down, annoyed, insulted. During Summer and Autumn, the splendid weather continued, robing the down-at-heel inhabitants and dilapidated villas, even the tree-denuded streets and gardens, with a golden halo. So expired 1943.

The year 1944 brought even greater trials. In February, invoking Article 52 of the Hague Convention, the Feldkommandantur ordained that "the civil male population between the ages of 16 and 60, without distinction of condition or profession, be requisitioned in the service of the German Authorities for labour in the vicinity of their places of residence; the sort of work, its importance and duration to be determined by the military Commanders on the spot." As most of the able-bodied men were already employed, many directly by the Germans or in the repair shops and factories working for them, this meant that youths had to abandon studies, old men their gardens, and that those accustomed to sedentary occupations had to turn out for work for which they were unfit. The Todt Organisation had already covered every yard of coast with fortifications. What then was the meaning of the new order? This soon became evident when unwilling squads were set to work digging trenches on the beaches and in the sandy soil of Chiberta. Pointless work which the night-winds undid, if not the sea or the rain. Nor did the soldier guards press the workers hard. Apparently, all the Germans wanted was to keep constant check on all the men.

On Monday 27 March, in the early afternoon of a bright sunny day, came the blow that in the brief space of half-an-hour turned Biarritz into a shambles and spread ruin through the town. Till then all that Biarritz had seen of the war was the occasional silhouette of a cruiser on the horizon or aircraft in the sky. Once an Italian submarine was chased right up the Adour[26] and bombed at quayside in Bayonne. There had been numerous alarms at night when mine-laying craft appeared off the estuary to obstruct the traffic in mineral ores between Spanish ports and Bayonne. Houses would shake when mines exploded. Occasional Royal Navy shells whined overhead to explode inland. As one saw the airfield at Parme extended and coming into use for training purposes, one felt that some day it would be bombed. That day had come.

The Allied planes, about a hundred in all, appeared in four waves from seaward some fifteen minutes after the sirens sounded. German anti-aircraft batteries immediately opened a fairly heavy fire which at first was ineffective. The attackers kept formation, circled to make

26. River passing through Bayonne.

reconnaissance, then began to unload over Parme. The adjoining railway station of La Négresse, where the Biarritz branch line joins the main Paris-Madrid trunk line, remained untouched. Nor did they attack Bayonne station with its marshalling yards and mineral dumps, the iron foundry at Le Boucau, the bridges, rail and road over the Adour, the Latécoère airplane works, or the Blancpignon powder factory, all tempting targets in full view. Despite the falling fragments from the barrage, and forgetful that Biarritz itself with its batteries and hotel-barracks might also become a target, people hung out of windows and stood on doorsteps and balconies to get a better view of the Allied Squadrons. And so it transpired towards the end of the raid when some 200 fragmentation bombs, as counted by the municipal authorities, fell on the town. Several hotels where Germans had headquarters, including the Kommandantur, suffered severely, as did adjacent streets, in particular the rue Mazagran. A train was set on fire in the railway station. Many roofs were smashed and at least half the glass in the town shattered. Among the places most heavily strafed was the Place St. Eugénie. The bandstand there received a direct hit; no longer would German music be played while pale-faced workers from the Reich, brought on tour by 'Strength through Joy' cars, strolled about.

Biarritz's Civil Defence Services, long since organised, got to work without delay. The wounded were hastily carried to aid-posts and the few available ambulances were employed in rushing the severely wounded to the numerous private nursing homes and hospitals in Biarritz and Bayonne. Unfortunately, many of the wounded bled to death before help could reach them. 105 bodies of civilians were recovered in the streets or among the ruins. Victims were being discovered four days after the bombing, witness a dying four-year-old child beside its dead parents. There were many sad cases demonstrating once again the lottery that is life. A lady from Pau, who had left her children to attend the funeral of her father-in-law in Biarritz, was killed as she returned from the ceremony. Two girls went out for a country walk. One did not want to go but was prevailed upon by the other. Together they walked to their death in a country lane. A well-known Biarritz cabby was on the stand in front of the railway station, both master and steed mere spectres of their former selves, when the first Allied aircraft appeared. Pegasus, abandoning his dejected droop, kicked himself free from traces and shafts and disappeared down a side street. Recovering from his surprise, Jehu set off in pursuit of his precious partner, regardless of falling flak. He soon caught him but nothing could persuade the beast to set his face towards the station. When, once the bombardment was over, the cabby was able to lead his trembling pal back to the vehicle, they found it riddled with glass from the marquee overhead. Horse-sense once more!

How many Germans were killed is not known. A number of corpses in uniform were laid out in the crypt of St. Eugénie church. Workmen sent to clear up the ruins of Parme said dead Germans were numerous there.

A public funeral service for the dead from the three parishes was held around the bandstand in the *Jardin Public* in front of the railway station. In long rows, coffins of French and some Germans lay side-by-side on the gravel. Above cross, cassock and uniform, above professed or private sentiment, Death, the great leveller, presided.

After this tragedy more trenches were dug in private gardens and life in Biarritz slumped to its dreariest. There were only five months to go to the liberation but no one could know it. In June came the great news of the *débarquement*[27] in Normandy. It at once made a difference because although the Basque sailor-folk never thought that the British would make an attempt to land on their remote, rocky, tide-swept coast, the Germans apparently did, and had troops ready. However, once the Landing had taken place, the German High Command appeared both to have assessed its importance and read the consequences correctly. The Aviation School trainee pilots on the triangle Mont-de-Marsan, Lescar and Biarritz, packed up immediately and went to Hamburg. Troop reserves to repel any attack from the sea also moved away. As the Normandy beachhead extended and fighting became fiercer, the drain continued and grew in momentum until, barely eight weeks

27. Landing.

later, German establishments were reduced to a mere skeleton of posts, mainly holding strategic points. Generals and their staff remained in Pau and Bayonne but they had little or no troops left to command. This was the opportunity the Resistance movement, with its army of Maquis, had been eagerly awaiting.

Throughout the southwest of France the Germans seemed to have pitched on 21 August as a sort of 'D' Day in reverse. On that day the retreat began south of the Adour. For several weeks previously, lines of communication all along the Pyrenees were continuously cut by the Maquisards, whose numbers and aggressiveness increased day-by-day, as parachuted arms and munitions became available. There could be no question for the Germans of entraining the remaining garrisons. They had to hoof it. So the good people of Biarritz stared at little companies of frontier guards, customs officers and sailors pushing babies' prams used as hand-carts or trailers, foot-sore and weary under the August sun, coming to rest under the Arcades. There they flung themselves down, pulling off jack boots to ease sore feet, not caring who looked on, nor what the onlookers might think of the Army of the Reich. The Germans in Biarritz had been busy for several days rounding up bicycles, not only taking them from owners in the streets but searching houses from garret to cellar. Anyone wearing a wristwatch stood a good chance of losing it, for the Germans were openly thieving from passers-by.

The night of 21 to 22 August 1944 will long be remembered by the inhabitants of the southern quarters of Biarritz. Before dusk, German patrols began warning all inhabitants of the Côte des Basques and Beau Rivage districts to retire several kilometres distant, leaving the doors and windows of their houses open, announcing that fortifications would be blown up after dark, causing terrible explosions. Many people obeyed and spent an uncomfortable night in the open. In fact, the Germans did not blow up the fortifications but only the big naval guns in the batteries and the large ammunition dump in the Sanitorium for Children at the head of the Côte des Basques. They set fire to the Sanitorium and it was burning and exploding most of the night. Several adjacent villas were wrecked and some civilians killed or wounded. Biarritz was lucky because the damage might have been much worse had there been one large explosion instead of piecemeal ones.

The bicycle thefts were much resented. During the night tin tacks were strewn along the Biarritz-Bayonne road with the result that, when the Germans set out on Tuesday morning, most of their tyres were soon punctured. At the St. Leon crossroads near Bayonne, the enraged Germans shot a man seen stooping on the roadway; a poor devil who was picking up tacks (unavailable in shops), not strewing them. At the first discharge he fell wounded, so they propped him up against a wall and finished him off under the eyes of his wife and daughter.

After this savage outburst, the column, covered by a rear guard of truculent Kriegsmarines, continued its way down the avenue leading to the great bridge over the Adour. At the river, the useless bicycles were unloaded and flung into the swift flowing waters. With them went much petty loot which the overladen and dispirited *feldgrau* could not carry. Thus tamely retreated northwards the remains of the arrogant hosts who had marched in so proudly fifty months previously. The withdrawal of the Germans was dogged, not only by sniping bands of Maquisards, but also by a persistent Biarritz luggage porter whose handcart they had carried off and, with it, his means of livelihood. He retrieved the property at Capbreton, twenty miles away.

After the main body of Germans had left, a motorcycle and sidecar carrying three Germans came rushing up the road from St. Jean de Luz. At Quesnel crossroads they asked the way to Bayonne and were promptly mis-directed. On discovering their mistake, they barricaded themselves in a villa, soon to be surrounded by Maquisards. A lively fusillade ensued until some Algerian Tirailleurs, from the prisoners' camp at Beyris, arrived on the scene and by fine marksmanship shot two of the Germans. The third surrendered.

Such was the ignominious end of the Germans in Biarritz – to provide a few moments of revenge for Arab tribesmen, free once more after four years' bondage.

Chapter 9

The Gentle Hun

The war experience of the British Colony on the Côte d'Argent makes for a tragic tale. Like many such stories, it began quietly enough. For several months after the occupation of the Basque country by the Germans, the 200-odd British residents, mostly elderly, who had decided to stay in France, continued to live normally enough; those who possessed homes maintained all their routines of daily life; those who had jobs kept them; and governesses and clerks, young and old, remained in employment. They had avoided the upheaval of sudden departure, the discomforts of a journey into the unknown and the hazards entailed. As time passed, it appeared to them that they had made the right decision, one that would spare them all the uncertainty of an unknown future.

Over cups of tea in the *patisseries,* still well supplied, they felt inclined to commiserate with friends and relatives who had left abruptly. Life was pleasant enough, the summer weather glorious. The American Consul and his wife, from being delightful friends had now become faithful protectors, dispensing the monthly allowances which eased monetary worries and who were always happy to use their good offices with the Kommandant, a dapper aristocrat, outwardly inscrutable but reputedly benevolent. The only negative was the obligation to report at the Kommandantur every morning at 8 a.m., though sometimes if one sent one's card by a servant or friend, the Germans did not mind.

To the Kommandantur, installed at the Town Hall, the energetic rode up on bicycles whilst others came in pony-traps or horse-drawn carriages, full of shopping parcels and guarded by Toby or Tom ready to yap at one and all, the *feldgrau* included. It was hardest, of course, on the older people for 8 a.m. German time was only 6 a.m. by the sun, although they sometimes found compensation in the opportunity

c. 1884. L to R: Alice, mother Mary, Emilie and Ernest.

c. 1889. Siblings L to R: Alice, Emilie and Ernest.

c. 1910. Ernest with sister Emilie.

On mobilization August 1914 with 14ème Compagnie du 23ème Territorial d'Infanterie before transfer to Corps of Interpreters and being assigned to Post Office Rifles (8th London Regiment).

Portrait of de Caux by Mildred Stapley Byne, Madrid, c. 1921.

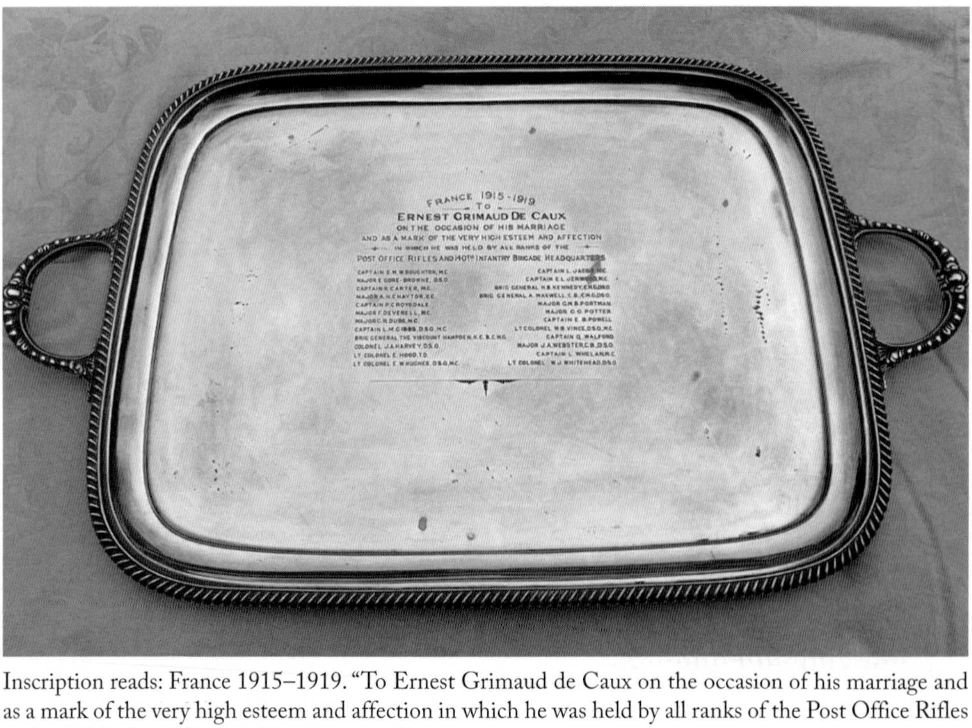

Inscription reads: France 1915–1919. "To Ernest Grimaud de Caux on the occasion of his marriage and as a mark of the very high esteem and affection in which he was held by all ranks of the Post Office Rifles and 140th Infantry Brigade Headquarters."

De Caux (second left front standing row) with French Army colleagues Great War. Photographer A. Kloubnikoff, Berck-Plage (Pas-de-Calais)

c. June 1918 with 140th Infantry Brigade Officers. Brigadier General H.B. Kennedy, CMG, DSO, has hands on de Caux's shoulders.

Republican militias in Madrid in 1936 at the beginning of the Civil War. (*Bridgeman images*)

International Brigades marching to the defence of Madrid. (*Alamy*)

French guards control flood of refugees crossing from Spain at Le Perthus (Pyrénées Orientales), 1939. (*Bridgeman images*)

General Franco takes salute, Nationalist victory parade, Madrid, 18 May 1939. (*Alamy*)

Refugees fleeing Paris, 1940. (*Getty Images*)

German defences on Biarritz beachfront. (*Alamy*)

Maison Blanche – Gestapo prison where de Caux was held for three weeks in early 1943.

c. 1950. De Caux by the plaque commemorating the re-opening and re-naming of the main Dublin bridge by his grandfather, Sir James W. Mackey.

c. 1950. L to R: With sister Alice and wife Olive.

c. 1958. With his niece, Maureen Eliet, on the Wicklow coast.

for café au lait and a croissant, or just a little harmless gossip on the benches nearby.

Nevertheless, the shadow of the sinister swastika (that vile variant of the ancient emblem of the Basques), displayed on flag-masts and posters, lay over everything. The passage of Hitler on his way to meet General Franco at Hendaye brought a foretaste of German ruthlessness. On 22 October 1940 all British subjects were suddenly rounded up at the Casino Municipal. Summoned, children included, for what they supposed would be just one more showing of documents, they found themselves snared, with armed guards at every exit.

A burly German major, fitting the type with cropped head and deeply scarred neck, sat at the table in the middle of a vast Salle des Fêtes with loads of chairs on either side of him. For five long hours, with the help of an interpreter, he examined and questioned his victims, passing them from one group of chairs to the other. Like sifting sands in an hourglass they passed, one by one, mere tools of fate. A French Police Inspector, with his piles of dossiers, looked on impassibly. A few Irish were sent away grinning. The long wait was very tiring for the children, of whom some were babes in arms, and for the elderly, huddled on the hard chairs. There was a blaze of light, for the great chandeliers were full on and even the stage was incongruously lit up. Outside, the sky was overcast with the makings of an Atlantic storm. The wind howled and drifting spray dashed against the windows. The waiting victims gazed at the desolate scene of breakers crashing on the deserted beach. For the waves, time counted not; they pounded away implacably as the cogs of the German machine began to grind yet another lot of unfortunates in its grip. As each subject of His Majesty was deprived of his passport and as the precious little blue book with the Royal Arms, embossed in gold, was flung on to the heap on the table, a link seemed to snap; despondency set in.

The only interruption to the morning's long proceedings was when Graf von Dietrich, the Kommandant, appeared. Orderlies stamped loudly and examining Officers sprang to attention as if suddenly stung from below. Graf was chided by Spanish friends who had entertained him and who could not understand how the blameless and ancient retainers who had served Grandees with quiet confidence for a generation or more came suddenly to be classed as dangerous enemies of the all-powerful Reich.

From the Casino, the British Colony, including nuns rounded up from their convents, were conveyed to the Hotel Continental, the war hospital. There, without any personal items they might have needed, they were confined and herded in wards while agents of the Gestapo came several times during the night for roll-call and to make sure no one had escaped. An early evening meal of cabbage and garlic sausage had been a foretaste of coarser and less plentiful food to come.

The windows of the Continental look across to the Carlton, an Officers' hotel, and to the Palais, where the Empress had resided and which now served as a headquarters of a Corps Commander. For three days the imprisoned British chafed under the indignities and discomforts heaped on them. All they could see of Biarritz was the uninspiring sight of German Officers stalking in and out of the hotels, and the old tram, its pristine cream paint soiled and grimy, lumbering by. Then, as soon as Hitler had headed North again, they were set free as suddenly as they had been arrested. A couple of days later they had their passports returned.

Safely back home, something of their former optimism returned. Bridge and tea parties were resumed. One and all, with the steadfastness borne of custom immemorial, began to look forward to Christmas. They were counting without the Gestapo. On the night of Thursday 5 December, they were surprised by the sight and sound of jack boots, sharp orders, massive battle helmets dripping rain, and gleaming arms. All this paraphernalia to round up harmless old men, women and young children. In one room where the grim soldiers broke in, a wife was weeping beside the body of her dead husband. "You must nevertheless come", they said. A French doctor present asked: "Do you want the dead man also?" A septuagenarian invalid lady living alone in a cottage near Arcangues[28] was roused in the night. You are not fit

28. Basque village near Biarritz.

to walk, pronounced a German medical officer, but you can be carried. Bedclothes were wrapped round a frail body and it was placed on a stretcher and taken away, with an old Basque servant, on her knees, pleading in vain that her mistress be spared. "What harm can an old woman like me do to you", asked the lady as the Germans carried her away, adding indomitably "not but that I would down you if I could". Then the heart that had been stout in spirit failed, and so, instead of bringing her to the train, they dumped her body at Bayonne Hospital. A nonagenarian, a helpless cripple, and a few lunatics, were spared. A Scot cheated Himmler of his prey at the last moment by collapsing and dying under the eyes of his would-be gaolers.

Mr McWilliams, the American Consul, went to the station to see them off but, though indignant about the whole matter, he could do nothing to alleviate their fate. Uncertainty as to their eventual destination greatly increased their anxiety. Many believed they were being taken to Germany. The journey lasted four days, the convoy crawling along, blinds drawn, picking up additions on the way, halting for interminable hours in sidings. Four cruel days and nights of bitter cold during which the elderly sat miserably on the hard wooden benches, children quarrelled, one and all filthy. A baby was born but both mother and child died on the jolting floor above the clamouring iron wheels of the carriage.

Finally, a halt came at Besançon, a snowed-up frontier town into which many of the prisoners, stiff and weary as they were, stumbled rather than walked. A great many had to be moved to hospital where, within a week, several died. The camp was a barracks, last occupied by French Colonial troops. As the column passed the gates, someone began to sing God Save the King and it was to the solemn tune of the National Anthem that the exhausted group came to rest. To rest indeed! The filthy straw left by the former occupants remained unchanged. There was no other bedding. Rats ran around, including over the kitchen utensils. There was not much water for washing. The latrines were out in the open. There were to be many fractures of arms and legs as various members of the group made their way across frost-bound yards in the dark. Dysentery set in. The dreadful conditions in the camp drew expressions of horror from several German officers. The deportation en masse was Himmler's doing apparently, and responsible members of the Army did not like being involved. Some Officers, however, took another view. One of these, walking through an unheated ward where the inmates sat about in despair, remarked airily: "So, living in idleness and luxury!" When matters were at their worst, RAF planes appeared and smoke-wrote COURAGE across the wintry sky.

Among the interned at Besançon, nuns alone numbered over four hundred, belonging to some seventy different Religious Orders. There was a venerable Poor Clare who had not broken cloister for 35 years and a 19 year old novice of the Paulites (Sisters of Charity), a cheery little soul from Glasgow, as well as a Canadian Bishop. The Religious were treated the same as the other prisoners, with only the ill or very infirm attaining the relative haven of the Hôpital St. Jacques. These Religious Orders could, had they been allowed, have brought welcome reinforcement to the overworked staff of the French Sisters of Charity.

In the unexpected occurrences that life bestows, old acquaintances met; a lady from Biarritz fell into the arms of a favourite golf partner who had long since left the sunny South to reside at Boulogne but who had failed to escape across the Channel. There were many tragic or just pitiable cases of foreigners caught in the net of British nationality: a little French woman, widow of an English Sergeant of 1914, whose whole life had been dedicated to bringing up his son, became paralytic under the shock of being abruptly separated from her boy; or the Persian lady murmuring endlessly "I am not Engleesh".

International Red Cross Inspectors arrived and conditions improved a little. The parcels from England, bringing warm clothing and tea, were a great boon. Nevertheless, the climate, coupled with the spartan conditions, were more than the elderly and infirm, weakened as they were, could withstand. There were many deaths. Among the victims destined to pass obscurely from camp to graveyard was the modest officer whom André Maurois immortalised as "Colonel Bramble". Peace to this gallant uncomplaining soul!

At the beginning of February 1941, as suddenly as had been their arrest, came release for all those over 65 as well as the certified invalids below that age. The camp at Besançon was condemned and the interned were removed to Vittel where a large hotel of the *station balnéaire*[29] was made ready to receive them.

For those released, the journey back to Biarritz contrasted with the journey up. It was effected in the charge of Red Cross workers and those who had the money were allowed to travel first class and even hot *café au lait* could be obtained. To one of this group, a German worker, having begun to boast as to how plentifully they were supplied, drew the courageous rejoinder: "Yes, since you take it all from the unfortunate French".

By the end of February the last of the freed exiles had returned to the Pays Basque. They came home to find the mild weather of an early Spring with daffodils, primroses, mimosa and heather abloom. Privations, however, had been too severe and the shock to ravished physiques too great. "I died in the train", said one elderly Englishman to his daughters as they helped him, legs swollen to twice their normal size, up the home stairs. He lived on for a few months but then, one night, after a pleasant day in his garden in view of the coastal mountains of La Rhune and the Jaizequibel,[30] he died. His wife, still convalescing from an injury, and who had accompanied him to Besançon, followed not long afterwards. Though a French woman, and knowing no English, she had been proud to suffer for England. Miss B, a sprightly octogenarian who saved up her parcels "to regale my friends in Biarritz" lived long enough to see her ambition fulfilled but her overstrained heart gave up one day as she tackled the long hill leading to her home.

The Germans interned both mistresses and maids. More of the former returned than the latter, owing to difference in age, but separation proved no obstacle to faithfulness in service. Pathetic notes from those still imprisoned to those now free, accompanied by little parcels, would

29. Spa.
30. Mountains of the Basque country.

find their way from Vittel to Biarritz with a few spoonfulls of tea, a scrap of bacon, a pot of jam.

Parcels from England to the internees gained such a reputation that, as conditions worsened to pre-starvation levels all over France, it became debateable as to whether life inside or outside the camp was the more endurable; so relative is everything in life.

A year after the deportation some eighty British were all that remained of the colony. They had lost their protector, Mr McWilliams, the American Vice-Consul. Those who owned villas had substituted vegetable patches for lawns and were cutting down trees and shrubberies for fuel. With telephones cut off, wireless sets confiscated, forbidden to enter the Bridge Club, obliged to be indoors before dark, unable to dispose of their bank accounts, life had become a long penance.

So, the third winter of the war, the second under the heel of the Germans, dragged on. For Southwest France, it was a severe winter with biting winds which cut to the bone. As February 1942 was ending, the remnants of the colony were rounded up once more. As before, the bolt descended quite suddenly. With 24 hours warning to be ready (hand luggage only, food for 3 days), the 'last guard', some sixty strong of the former colony of 200, were embarked at noon on Friday 27 February, in a third class German coach labelled Breslau. As had been the case fifteen months previously, there were friends at the station to wish them farewell, bringing small presents and bunches of the first Spring flowers. The former Mayor of Biarritz was also present. Although, among the travellers, the enthusiast who had taken a cage-full of canaries to Besançon was absent, a girl leading a cheerful black cocker spaniel maintained British traditions. Nuns fingered their rosaries, among them a frail figure from India and a robust Canadian representing the Empire. Stolid German officers passed the roll-call. A French Inspector checked off each name. After processing, the prisoners climbed into the forbidding coach awaiting them.

Among the departing travellers was a small child in a soiled, woollen knitted suit. Little Lilian, though barely three and of French nationality to boot, was already a veteran of Besançon. This waif was going off a second time so as not to become a worse waif. Such are the contradictions, absurd and cruel, bred of war. When Italy came into the war in June 1940, Lilian's mother, wife of a Frenchman, daughter of an English veteran of 1914–18, and living in Nice, had begged her parents to take her baby to safety. So, this one-armed grandfather and his wife, with the little bundle in its perambulator, had trekked across France to Biarritz, which at the time appeared the safest spot in the country. But, a few weeks later, the Germans marched into Biarritz without the Italians having reached Nice. When the emergency arose in 1940, the grandparents took Lilian to Besançon rather than abandon her. When the mother heard of the plight of her little one, she tried to cross into occupied France but was arrested and sent back to Nice, the Armistice terms containing no provision for Lilian or small victims like her.

The second exile of the English had evidently been prepared with cruel foresight. The old German third class carriage had been brought from afar. It was one of those country coaches for short journeys. Owing to a central corridor, none of the narrow seats made of hardwood were long enough for lying down. There was neither water nor heating. After three days and nights in this prison, the trainload of exiles finally reached St. Honoré les Bains, a small spa town in central France. No warning of their arrival had been given and nothing was ready to receive them. Hastily, the hotel Bellevue was opened by the French Authorities after being closed for two years. Owing to frozen pipes, there was no water. The beds had no blankets or sheets. Into these freezing, damp apartments, the perishing British settled down as best they could to a third consecutive night of misery. Many became sick. Old Mr L. died. Little Lilian, both grandparents seriously ill, had to be sent to the local creche, there to develop peritonitis.

There were no Germans actually at St. Honoré but they turned up once a week to count their victims. The area is sometimes called *La Sibérie de la France.*

One elderly lady, on Friday 27 February, was not on the convoy for St. Honoré. Nor was she at home. Miss H. had survived Besançon with the firm resolve never again to go on such a journey if she could help it. When the round-up for the second internment took place, Miss H. was not notified. Why she could not understand because she counted herself at least as active as many of her contemporaries. But, respectful of authority, even German, she went round to the Kommandantur and asked if she also should prepare. There, one of the clerks told her that, as she had not been notified, she need not worry. But worry she did, for the worst would surely be if, at the last moment, she had to leave her little flat in a hurry without having time to put away her treasures: a gilt clock and a plaster owl, perched, pen-in-claw, presiding over the daily routine of the septuagenarian. That would be truly dreadful. So, on the Friday morning, Miss H. rose betimes and departed, basket in hand, to the cemetery. That, she thought, would be the last place where they would think of making a last hour search. Moreover, the railway lines skirted the cemetery so she counted on a good view of the train as it passed and to know when it would be quite safe to return home. The cemetery, with its many good old county names of English, Scotch and Irish, its resounding titles of Spanish Grandees and Russian Princes, its tongue-twisting Basque names, proved quite interesting. Midday passed and one, two and three o'clock. Miss H., ensconced between cypress and marble, ate her hard-boiled egg and took a draft of red wine. That made her feel better.

At last, towards 3.30 p.m., it came rumbling and scraping round the bend. There was no mistaking it by one who had been to Besançon. The comfortable green coach for officers in front; the battered, old third class, blinds down, in the middle; and the coach for guard troops behind. Grinding and groaning the convoy passed. Miss H. stared at it, then got up and made for home. She felt rather sick at the thought of friends huddled in their prison-carriage, affronting an immediate ordeal and the hazardous future once more, with only one certainty, the literally dead one that the journey would end for some in the grave. Had not Besançon cost thirty lives in the first week?

Once back in her tiny little flat, Miss H. felt better. Solitude did not frighten the gentle-voiced old lady who had long since grown used to facing life's trials alone. The first glance went to the wall where stood the three noble heads of Les Chantres. Then she set about making a cup of tea, or what stood for it. The owl looked on gravely. The gilt clock chimed the hour. As Miss H. busied herself, "The Campbells are coming, tra-la tra-la" kept echoing in her head, confused but hope-fraught echo of the Kommando exploits France was beginning to ring with those days. Miss H., however, finally had to pack her treasures and depart when the Germans made a final combing of coastal areas. This time the exiles were allowed to travel by the regular train service, unescorted, to inland areas.

At long last, liberation came in August 1944. By then, less than twenty of the original 200 were all that remained. Some, alas, were bedridden in their homes, attended by devoted servants whose wages were long overdue, for the allowances received monthly through the Swiss Legation were barely sufficient to keep body and soul together.

The good people of Biarritz had not forgotten their English friends and patrons. The doyenne of the survivors, old Mrs B., an indominable octogenarian who had lost three sons in 1914–18, was overjoyed when they sent her a large Union Jack to hoist over her villa. Colonel F., gamely walking along with the help of two sticks in front of Biarritz Bonheur,[31] was beset by shop girls rushing to embrace him. For one horrible moment, he remembered that it is the custom for Frenchmen also to embrace, so he hobbled away before the threat of bristling beards. But the greatest satisfaction came when the Municipality hastened to replace, on its desecrated pedestal, the bronze medallion of Queen Victoria which someone had saved from the Germans. However, there could be no Thanksgiving Service at the British Church. For one thing there was no Chaplain; for another the Church had been all but destroyed by British bombs. The night before the Germans left they exploded an ammunition dump on the Côte des Basques. Resulting from this, one of the oldest British residences in Biarritz was burnt to the ground. The charred walls of l'Hermitage, visible from far out at sea, remains a fitting emblem of the havoc wrought amidst the British Colony of Biarritz.

31. Department store in the centre of Biarritz.

Chapter 10
In Prison

The fate English friends had foretold for me at Bordeaux, in June 1940, was not realised until March 1943 when, one evening between eight and nine agents of the Gestapo entered our house, a small villa named Etche Churria (basque for White House). I had just finished reading a fortnight-old number of the *Weekly Times*, the only foreign newspaper, apart from an *Illustrated London News*, to reach my hands since the Armistice. When the bell rang and I heard the loud voice by the hall door, I laid the paper down on a stand beneath the wireless set and rose to meet a disagreeable German, dressed in plain clothes and accompanied by his interpreter, a Swiss, who was the former employee of a Biarritz business firm.

Having examined my identity card, the German asked me my profession and what I had been doing before the war. I told him the simple truth, that I was *The Times* Correspondent in Madrid and Paris. "You are arrested" I was told. My wife looked on anxiously. "You may collect your toilet necessaries, a change of linen and some food", explained the interpreter. "Take an overcoat", he advised. He accompanied me upstairs, thus leaving the Gestapo fellow alone in my study, with all my books.

Out of the corner of my eye, as I left the room, I saw him pick up a framed photograph of the Staff of 140 Infantry Brigade BEF, in which I had served in 1915–1918. I was sure his eyes would soon drop to the pile of papers with the incriminating number of *The Times* lying on top. As soon as I could I whispered to my wife: "Go down and see what that fellow is up to". Down she went and soon I could hear her expostulating voice and angry tones. Weeks afterwards I learned that she found him kicking the enamelled woodstove. When she protested he shouted: "That is where you burn the documents". Then he opened the bookcase and became absorbed in the rows of books on the Spanish Civil War.

I was conveyed to the Maison Blanche, another white house, a former villa which had been transformed into a prison for those awaiting trial. In the Wardroom my watch and everything but my overcoat were taken from me and I was locked into the *cabanon*,[32] a cell next to the central heating plant in the basement. It contained three army cots and I set myself down on one of them. It was a horrid sound to hear the keys rasping in the rusty lock. The heat was oppressive, but I managed to unlatch a small window near the ceiling. It opened on to the garden. Almost immediately a voice asked through the door: *"Pourquoi vous ouvrir, Monsieur?"* to which I replied: *"Parceque j'ai trop chaud."* The *Monsieur* surprised me. The light in the cell was then extinguished from outside and I was left in peace.

My reflections on the situation were not at all agreeable. As a rule, when arrests were made, domiciliary perquisitions followed immediately, and they were ruthless and thorough.

I imagined the mantle mirrors being torn down, the floorboards ripped up, even the drains opened and examined, not to speak of every chest, cupboard and trunk being emptied out – the fate of several villas known to me. What a night my unfortunate wife and relatives must be having, I thought, and what a mixed bag for the Gestapo, for Spanish as well as British and American refugees leaving Biarritz had deposited personal belongings of all sorts. There was also the luggage of a former Military Attaché, the family linen and silver of a Consul, not to mention sets of frontier maps, the MM.SS. of a good part of this book and some copies of a fortnightly *News Bulletin* I had been compiling for limited circulation for over two years. There was the typewriter on which it had been written as well as materials for writing in secret inks. In a word, now that I was trapped, I had to acknowledge that from the German point of view I seemed fair game. It was not a nice feeling.

32. A 'cabanon', normally an outdoor shed, usually built of wood – but taking on another meaning here.

What worried me most was all the trouble it might cause my family and the dire prospect that my wife might also be arrested. My most immediate problem was to invent some story to account for the presence in my house of that *Weekly Times*, so to cover the tracks of those who gave it to me. Like the above-mentioned *Illustrated London News*, it had been brought from San Sebastián by a German and had then passed through various hands before reaching me. I could hardly tell them that it had been purchased by the Chief of the Gestapo, though that was actually the truth. The thought flashed through my mind that I might have been set up. Somehow the dreary night passed. When day dawned, contrary to expectations, I was not brought up for immediate interrogation. Instead, I was removed from the *cabanon,* given two tattered blankets and bundled into Room No.2 on the second floor, after the warder had stood over me whilst I read a list of rules posted at the entrance. Rule No.1 forbade absolutely prisoners to talk to each other about the circumstances or reasons for their arrest.

When the door closed and I turned to inspect my new quarters, I saw there were already three inmates who were gazing at me with kindly eyes. The one nearest, big-nosed, short and stocky, said to me in low tones, for we could be heard from the outside: I am Gaston, a white Jew, been here 44 days and am *chef de chambrée*.[33] Edmond there – he pointed to a large-boned, fine-featured figure with bare feet thrust into *sabots*[34] – complained that the soup at the Regina was bad, while René here – a dark Landais[35] in a blue jersey – is the victim of a treacherous woman. What have you done? Chiefly the affair of an English accent, I replied, although neither in my case nor in theirs was it that simple. What about rule No.1 , I asked. They laughed.

This introduction over, I was pointed toward the best of the three empty cots, shown how to tease the straw so that it should be less bullet-hard, and advised to prepare for a hot shower, that is to say to undress, for it was washing day – a treat not to be missed – and each

33. Head room-mate.
34. Clogs.
35. 'Landais' – from the department of the Landes, stretching from Bordeaux to Bayonne.

room must be ready to dash out when the word came. The secret with the warders is to kow-tow in all small matters, I was told – never to smoke or keep one's cap on in their presence and to spring about cheerfully as if one were overjoyed to be living in their beastly prison. At that price, explained Gaston, No.2 has gained a reputation which earns us many small favours: they do not spy on us continuously and at mealtimes we get second helpings if there are any surplus rations.

I found that, besides the weekly bath, one could wash *ad lib* in a *cabinet de toilette* with running water off our room. There was a Northwest window and an East window, giving air and light, though boarding fixed outside the barred windows and sloping upwards and outwards cut off most of it. Through chinks in the boarding we caught our only view of the outside world. One could see a bit of the street in front of the entrance to the Maison Blanche and a corner of the Public Gardens facing the Railway Station. How nonchalant the life of the free appears to those deprived of liberty. One could see children playing, the bent figure of a former Ambassador in London stooping to rest on a bench, girls tripping by, old women gossiping. Nearly all of them, as they passed, stopped to gaze at the villa with its boarded windows. One man shook his fist at it. These strangers became symbols for us prisoners – emblems of liberty. How eagerly we spied on their movements, watched their gestures; we, the powerless ones, locked six to a room. We were lucky for in other rooms the inmates numbered many more, packed like herrings. In all, some fifty men and as many women were cooped up in the Maison Blanche, a former boarding-house for a score of guests.

There was nothing to do but talk, play cards (forbidden), smoke, or just cogitate. We were allowed to purchase newspapers and reviews. A pile of German propaganda was stacked on the chimney-mantle. The papers, of course, gave only German news. The propaganda stuff was left untouched. To the amusement and somewhat to the contempt of my companions, I read it all carefully. It was lifeless. The real news came on Thursdays when Gaston and René talked with their wives for half an hour.

By pushing table and benches up against the cots, there was just room to pass. This gave space for six paces between the entrance door and the *cabinet de toilette*. In turn we took what exercise we could in this gangway. Twice a week only, while I was there, were we taken out for half an hour's exercise. Two files were formed, one for the able-bodied and the other for the invalids. The first group quick-marched or trotted around in a circle waving their arms in rhythmic gesture. The latter merely promenaded disconsolately. It was forbidden to speak, but prisoners nearest to each other managed to exchange *sotto voce* phrases passing on items of news. On the days when the women were allowed out, the yard was full of chatter. We could hear the shrill voice of their wardress Ilso, *la chatte,* shouting at them, and the men warders swearing, but to no avail.

The food question was settled by the Germans ordering the Secours National to supply rations. These were sent in a little cart from the cookhouse of the Restaurant du Maréchal, a sort of communal dining-hall. We prisoners got the same food as the customers of the restaurant but without having to pay for it. Not by any means bad food and decently cooked as well. Every Thursday our families were allowed to bring parcels and those among us whose interrogation had ended were allowed to talk with a visitor. Every day a pail of water, scrubbing brush and cloth were brought to our cell. On Saturdays, it was boiling water with disinfectant and we were expected to scrub the floor. This gave a lot of exercise because the space was so tight and the table and benches had to be piled on top of each other so as to free the floor. The servants at the Maison Blanche were two young Spaniards who had been caught smuggling at the frontier and condemned to a sentence of one year serving fellow prisoners. They seem scared stiff of the Germans. The warders were all Warrant Officers, men who had been severely wounded but not maimed. Monopatte limped, having lost several toes to the freezing temperatures of Russia. The others were able-bodied and all were armed with automatics. The Chief Warder was a regular from the Prison Corps of Berlin, and the Governor, a whiskered aristocrat, Count Volvich, who only very occasionally visited the prison.

The Germans called the Maison Blanche a detention hostel and, with an eye to propaganda, had made it a model of its kind. It was for many, however, but the ante-room to the sinister Fort du Ha at Bordeaux and internment or prison camps in Germany. All sorts of people were picked up to pass days, weeks, or months in this Gestapo hotel. While I was there it was full of real Jews, "White" Jews, tramps and aristocrats, a notary from Bayonne, old men and many boys caught trying to cross the frontier. During exercise one day, I exchanged a smile with the Marquis d'Arcangues and his son Guy. I already knew he was *in quod* for his first interrogation had taken place on the landing outside our cell and I had recognised his voice when he had exclaimed "I swear on my honour", amidst German jeers.

To all of us except Edmond the days seemed intolerably long. Edmond was having a rest cure and was making the best of it. He was a lonely soul, born unwanted and handed over to the Assistance Publique. Whilst serving in a cavalry regiment, a kick from a horse had ruptured his stomach. Despite this, he was forced to work for Todt on the fortifications for the Atlantic Wall. Based, along with hundreds of others, in the gutted Regina Hotel, he declared one day that the soup which they had been given was disgusting. "But I drink it", said the German NCO in charge. "It is only fit for pigs", retorted Edmond – "I will send you where it is better", shouted the enraged Sergeant, so I was arrested and brought here, explained Edmond, "Where indeed the soup is much better". I never saw an appetite for soup like Edmond's. On Thursdays, when we married men received our parcels, he would have a field-day drinking five or six plates of soup.

A couple of days after my arrival, in danced another Edmond, the postman of our street, a dapper little man. Accustomed to walking or cycling 20 miles a day, he suffered at first from enforced inaction and would prance frantically on the narrow gangway. His crime was that he had given an address to a young man who wanted to escape to Spain. As the days passed he became increasingly worried as he had had no news from his mother. Finally, one day, while looking out through one of the chinks in the boarding, he saw someone he knew pass by. Shinning up the window bars, he managed to attract his friend's attention and shout "Tell mother". His mind thus set to rest, Edmond, the postman, became another person. He could tell endless stories and, as he had all the gossip of Biarritz at his fingertips, he proved a great acquisition for Room No.2.

Next arrived Paul, an immaculate figure in plus-fours and Byron shirt. He was a fur merchant in Paris and had done well over a contract of jackets for Germans in Russia. With the Spring came a longing for a holiday in the sunny South and a round of golf at Chantaco, the beautiful course at the foot of the Rhune mountain. So, Paul took a fortnight off and bought tickets for two to St Jean de Luz, himself and a *petite amie*. At Dax, German police asked for their papers. Parisians cannot enter the coastal zone. It was forbidden a fortnight ago, they were told. Oh, alright, said Paul, it really does not matter, we can have our holiday here; there are Roman baths. Hurry, Louisette, take down your hat. Not at all, said the Germans. You bought tickets for St Jean de Luz for some purpose. Go there. At St Jean de Luz, Paul and Louisette were arrested and sent to the Maison Blanche. Good-bye Chantaco. What can they do to us, asked Paul. Surely we will be set free tomorrow or the next day. We shall see, said Gaston, with a little tone of doubt in his voice. My wife was locked up here for seventeen days for one imprudent word. When the Germans were searching our house and pulled out all the clean sheets from the linen chest and began stamping on them, she uttered the word "brutes". But that was an insult, protested Paul, we have insulted no one. You have done worse, you have broken a rule, retorted Gaston.

Indeed, Paul and Louisette seemed fated to break rules for at that very moment came the sound of heel-tapping on the floor above. We stopped talking, a woman's voice could be heard calling: Paul, I hear your voice. How are you? Oh, what happiness, rejoined Paul, I am alright, among good friends (*we bowed).* Et toi, comment vas-tu? I'm also alright, the silvery voice replied. We are three here, but now, most of all, I'm delighted because I can talk to you. They did so, fairly often, until one day, when Paul was perched on the topmost cot addressing the ceiling in impassioned tones, the door suddenly flew open and the irascible Monopatte appeared. An awkward silence ensued, broken by frantic heel-tapping. A shrill voice demanded: What has happened, Paul, I can't hear you anymore. Paul gestured in despair while Monopatte crossed his arms and waited. "Continue Sir, continue Sir, Madam awaits. You not polite if you not answer", but Paul did not say a word. He was moved to another room and, thereafter, we saw him only at exercise-time, always smiling, always the most cheerful of us all.

Thinking about who would be the next to turn up was one of the ways of passing the time. In fact, we were wondering who would replace Paul when the door opened and a medium-sized young man was pushed in. His clothes were ragged and dirty and a huge shock of fine auburn hair topped a pink boyish face. We gave him a cigarette whilst he explained that he was a *rescapé*[36] from the Hôtel Edouard VII. There were nearly 100 in there, constantly beaten, lying on the floor, and given one ladle of soup a day. Most of them had been picked up whilst trying to escape to Spain, which was exactly what had happened to our new companion. He had endured more than a fortnight of starvation at the Edouard VII before being taken out with another young man and marched, handcuffed, to the Maison Blanche. On the way, a small crowd had gathered, but dispersed once the escort began to finger their rifles somewhat ostentatiously.

"Jean Dusek, a miner, but the Germans don't know that" was how he presented himself before asking if there were any means of his getting a wash. We showed him the cabinet de toilette and lent him a piece of soap. There was great splashing and scrubbing. When he reappeared, his shirt, washed and wrung out, was hanging on the top bars of the window. He had changed into a close-fitting black suit, the Sunday go-to meeting garb of all self-respecting coalminers, as I remember them, in the Béthune district in 1914–1918. I asked him if he knew

36. Survivor.

Mazingarbe,[37] for a long period our military base. Yes, he said. In the Maison de la Mine on the square by the rebuilt church, an English Sergeant and twelve men held out for two days after their comrades had gone. Stukas dive-bombed the building; they all died fighting. More unknown heroes.

Jean told us his story. His father was one of nine survivors of the original Czech Legion, formed at Bordeaux in 1916. An exploit of these men had been the capture of a corner of the Lens minefield towards the end of the war. Old Dusek, having suffered four wounds and been gassed, settled at Méricourt with his wife and family. There, Jean was born, French by nationality. He was 15 when the war came again to Artois. He showed the popular enthusiasm when the British marched through on their way to defending Belgium. Despondency, however, set in when, outflanked, outnumbered and bombed day and night, the same troops passed westward towards Dunkirk. "We had left the village and taken to the fields. I helped my father build a shelter in a haycock. My mother and sister were there. Two older brothers had left long since to join the Czech Forces in England. The Germans were not far away and we could hear machine-gun fire and shells flying about. A British Bren gun carrier came clattering down the road and had the misfortune to turn over in a ditch. My father and I helped get it back on the road. An officer thanked us, then looking at me said: 'If you want to come along, climb aboard'. I looked at my old father. 'Go along, sonny, go along', he said, but I could not bear to leave him and my family out there in the fields. 'I see you do not have the makings of a soldier,' called out the Officer as he rumbled off. I went back to the haycock. It began to rain but I could hear the fighting in the village continuing. My father lay out full length, exhausted. One of his fits seized him and he could not move. Amidst the racket some Germans appeared, sub-machine guns in hand. 'Hands up or we shoot'. 'Civilians' we shouted. They came forward, flashing torches in our faces, and ordered us back to the village. I had to carry my father

37. Mazingarbe, where the author spent some time during the 1914–18 war.

on my back some distance. I was tottering towards the village and only just managed to make it. I was glad I had remained with him because otherwise he would have been left in the field on his own. For three days and nights we remained confined in a house with other villagers. The Germans gave us food but forbade us to go out until they had cleared the district. There were many English stragglers trying to find their way to the coast and everyone was helping them.

"The Germans soon got the mines working again; the English had not been able to destroy the pitheads completely. I went back to work in the mines. We were bombed but nonetheless all the sympathy of the miners was with the crews overhead bombing us. I grew restless. Todt was recruiting and offering good pay. I had picked up German fairly easily so I joined them and was sent down South. It was strange to feel the warm sun in winter. Many Todt workers deserted and I heard Germans saying that at least 10,000 had crossed into Spain during the winter. A friend and I decided to go as well. We found a Basque who offered to get us across the Bidassoa at Biriatou[38] for 2000 francs. We went openly by train to St Jean de Luz. There our guide said it would be better to walk the remaining kilometres. At dusk we saw the river below us. 'Give me the money now', said our guide, 'and tomorrow at dawn I will put you across. It will be best to spend the night in this barn'. I protested: 'No, we will not give you the money until we have one foot in the water'. 'Into the barn anyway', said the guide. Germans were waiting for us there. We had been betrayed.

Jean told us this story unemotionally. He seemed a cool customer. He expected to be sent to the Russian front on forced labour. That night he slept like a log but in his sleep he kept moaning *"J'ai faim, J'ai faim"*.

Robert was the next to arrive, a Jewish commercial traveller living alone in a flat with a little cat. The day being warm he had doffed his overcoat and thrown it over his arm, thus momentarily hiding (oh heinous crime!) the large yellow star all Jews were obliged to display. Within ten minutes he was in custody. He had not been allowed to

38. 'Bidassoa': river marking the frontier with Spain. 'Biriatou' is a small village near the frontier.

go home for a change of clothing. What will become of my cat, he wailed. In the middle of the night Robert had a fainting fit. We rang the alarm bell, as authorised by the rules, and asked for a doctor. When the warder heard it was for the Jew he flew into a rage, told Robert to go to hell and slammed the door. The next morning he scowled horribly when he saw that Robert had recovered.

A second Jean came to us about the same time. When he entered, I thought he was a Spanish Red militiaman; pirate face, cropped head, thick woollen jersey, patched khaki drill trousers, hemp-soled sandals – all was there, only the rifle was missing. Sure enough he hailed from Spain, that is from Fernando Poo. He was a Luxemburger, employed as an analyst on that remote island – a humble soul working far away from home for reasons best known to himself. He had lived in that unpleasant climate for 15 years and had had no intention of leaving when the Spanish Police informed him one day that he had now become a German citizen and, accordingly, must return to his country to take out new identity papers. But can they not be sent to me here, he protested, declaring he had neither the money nor the desire to travel. At this point, the Civil Guard took charge of him and he was sent, via the Canary Islands, Cadiz, and Madrid, to San Sebastian, always protesting and trying by every means to delay his return. His journey had taken many months and he had been lodged in Spanish prisons the whole time.

Jean the Second had finally been accompanied from Madrid to the coast by two Civil Guards. One of them commented on the vagaries of fortune. You have no luck, he admitted, just like my brother. He was a Civil Guard like me, just the same, though we were not in the same regiment. I was stationed in the zone where Franco commanded. Franco won. My brother was in Madrid with the Republican Government. It lost. Now he is serving a 30 year sentence. It might just as well have been me. That is fate.

At San Sebastian the Guards brought Jean to the door of a building from a balcony of which hung the blood-red flag with the black Swastika. You are free now, they told him…. free to walk upstairs! In the office, a gentleman, dressed like an Admiral, was very polite and bade Jean welcome. You will be sent to Cologne, he said, where papers for all new naturalisations are issued. There is no longer any Duchy of Luxemburg and so we have been obliged to recall you, but it will be alright and you may return to Fernando Poo later if you wish. From San Sebastian, Jean was conducted in a German car to Hendaye, where he spent two days de-lousing at the sanitary camp the Germans had thoughtfully provided to clean up the Blue Division on its way to Germany and Russia. Thus he reached us bedraggled and discontented, but disinfected.

Days and weeks passed, and the tediousness of imprisonment was lightened only by the kaleidoscope of life that passed through our little room. One always hears of prisoners being quarrelsome. God knows that with the snoring of some and the habits of others we were a motley crew but, nonetheless, remained brothers in misfortune and shared out the parcels some of us received, as well as our tobacco. Common aversion to the Germans created a bond, which prisoners jailed by society presumably do not feel. That White House comradeship was a very real thing.

Uncertainty as to the fate of Etche Churria and my family, as well as the grim outlook for myself, made me thoroughly miserable during the first few days. Then, one morning, whilst spying through the chinks in the boarding, I saw my wife. She was walking with a light brisk step away from the Maison Blanche. There was no despondency in her demeanour and, obviously, she was free. My heart gave a great bound. The implied message from her demeanour meant so much to me. It seemed to indicate also that there had been no perquisition at Etche Churria. Given a few hours, I knew my wife could be relied upon to put away my manuscript and anything else of importance. A bottle of fresh milk[39] was brought up to me after her visit and this continued every day subsequently.

39. The author had an ulcer and it was important for him to sip some milk during the day.

Nevertheless, I waited in suspense for the interrogation. Every time the key turned in the lock, I jumped. "They are never in a hurry. They let one stew in one's juice", explained Gaston. Then, one afternoon, it came. I was ushered into a bare room with a table and chairs. A small dark young man, with the same interpreter who had come to my house, awaited me. He began by asking what seemed to be all sorts of irrelevant questions. Was I a Jew? Had I any Jewish ancestors? Who were my parents and grandparents? What property did I own? He asked me the same questions regarding my wife. I found these personal questions irritating in the extreme. What a prisoner wants to know is why he has been arrested and what he is charged with.

At last the charge came. We Germans know English life well, I was told, so we know that every *Times* Correspondent becomes *ipso facto* a member of the Intelligence Service. I was therefore a spy, an agent of Germany's enemies. Would I please state on what subjects I had supplied reports. Despite natural anxiety as to my possible fate, I almost laughed, so ludicrous did the German approach appear to me. I pointed out that their assumption as to the direct connection between the Intelligence Service and Printing House Square was quite incorrect. Moreover, I told them that it was almost three years since I had ceased all relations with *The Times*. I supposed, I told them, seeing that they had arrested me, that they had some definite facts on which to go, apart from their suspicions – some reprehensible activity on my part. 'Most certainly' replied the Gestapo official. 'You have, for instance, stated, in the presence of witnesses, one of whom has referred the matter to us, that Germany would surely be beaten and that the Russians would take Germans away to Russia and make them work to repair the destruction of Ukraine'. 'That,' I replied, 'is only an opinion and not of any great importance'. It is very important, replied the interrogator. 'You had better make a clean breast of it at once. Tell us what reports you made and to whom,' he insisted. 'I have nothing to say,' I stated with as much conviction and energy as I could muster. 'Well then, go back and meditate on it. Yours is a serious case and frankness might help you. Dissimulation is useless.' At this point I was brought back to the room.

I sat down and pondered it over. How much do the Germans really know? The footling little story about the conversation did not seem a serious accusation. It was so accurate in detail that it gave away who the Germans' informer was. There had only been four people present, three of whom were above suspicion, when I mentioned the Russian intention to make them rebuild Kharkov. Surely, if the Gestapo had any convincing evidence, they would have produced it at once. What could they gain by wasting time? But such was their reputation for astuteness and perversity that I could not quite feel reassured. The young man who interrogated me had not given the impression of being very experienced. Gaston did not know him; he had had to deal mainly with a big fellow nicknamed "the butcher", whose manner was insulting and who would, as often as not, knock his victim from one side of the room to the other with the blow of his fist.

The following day I was asked to give a written statement of my life in student days. Also, and somewhat surprisingly, I was taken out to see a doctor, who turned out to be a mild-mannered person. There, once more, I saw the hand of my wife. He asked me if I was still troubled with facial neuralgia. I replied that I was and mentioned the remedy I was taking. He advised that I continue taking it and gave an order for me to be supplied with another box.

A week later a second interrogation followed, but there was still nothing more in terms of accusations against me. This time it was an older official, a searching questioner. His main objective seemed to be to ascertain who were my friends and acquaintances. Give me a list of all the people you know in Madrid and Biarritz, he said, pushing pencil and paper toward me. That would take all day, I said, because I know everybody from the shoemaker to officials in high office. I am not interested in those, he said, so that session came to an inconclusive end.

A third time I was called to the sinister room. An elderly red-headed man with the prim manner of a Lutheran Minister reproached me for not confiding completely in German justice. I reminded him that I had admitted the truth of the conversation reported to them but could not go beyond that. Again, I was remanded. As I left the room he said in solemn tones: 'You have told some of the truth, but not all of it.' I made my way, wondering if they had put a thought-reader on me.

German justice indeed! That very morning, René had been tried and condemned to three years' hard labour, if the proceedings of a Court of five officers sitting in a Biarritz hotel, could be called a trial. René had been led off by two policemen. He returned an hour later, broken by emotion and furiously indignant. Words stuck in his throat. In the hall of the hotel, he had seen the witnesses for his defence, but they were never allowed into Court. The Judges heard only the accusation and then made their decision. Ren protested vehemently but no attention was paid to him when he shouted: 'My witnesses!'. On the way back, the German Military Police, who had seen it all, were indignant. They said to René: 'You write to our General. He'll put matters right.' We spent the afternoon concocting an appeal which René then laboriously copied out in his clumsy handwriting. He had been condemned solely on the evidence of a woman of ill repute who previously had been sentenced for perjury at Mont de Marsan Assizes and despite the fact that the French Court had communicated the condemnation to the German Courts Martial.

Everything has an end, even misery. One glorious April evening, after 22 days' captivity, I was turned out of the Maison Blanche as unceremoniously as I had been brought in. Towards 5 p.m., at the end of another tedious day, the Chief Warder appeared at the door and asked me to go with him, making signs that I was to bring my belongings with me. That spelt departure. But for where? My companions silently embraced me, not knowing whether I was to be congratulated or commiserated with, for many departures merely spelt transfer from one Gestapo hole to another, usually a worse one since the Maison Blanche was the best of them all, a homage, unconscious or not, paid by the Germans to the universal reputation of Biarritz as a civilised place.

I followed the Chief downstairs. In the Office, the Interpreter was seated at a desk. He rose and said: 'We have decided to set you free.' My watch, suitcase and other belongings were returned to me. Almost before I could realise what was happening, I found myself descending the steps to the street, free as air. I crossed the road, put down my suitcase, and from a spot where I knew I could be seen through those blessed chinks, cut a few senseless capers. It was one of those rare moments in life when one feels foolish through sheer joy. This silly *adieu* duly paid to the forlorn ones in No. 2, I walked home.

I feel sure it was my wife who got me out. The very next morning after my arrest she had begun to worry the Germans, defying them to produce evidence against me. She had stayed up all night 'cleaning up', and given what she knew, that in itself was a very courageous act. It had taken her four days to find out where I was because at both the Kommandantur and the Maison Blanche they had begun by lying to her. Once sure that I was in Biarritz she redoubled her efforts, confronting Volvich and the Gestapo Chiefs at their headquarters in Bayonne. They had tried to get her to give them a list of my friends. 'My husband would not approve of that,' she said, pushing pencil and paper away. 'One thing at least we have learnt,' they said to her, 'that neither you nor your husband love the Germans. You have no sympathy for us.' 'Sympathy is one thing, correctness another', was her sturdy reply. During her last visit she heard one official say it was useless continuing because they wouldn't get anything out of her.

She, however, was determined to get something out of them, so in one way or other kept returning to the charge, persistent though never impatient. The steady confidence and devotion she displayed impressed even those Huns. Good friends also helped.

Shortly after my release, a peremptory order from the Germans, giving us three days' notice, exiled us to the other zone.[40]

40. There were two zones – occupied and unoccupied. The author and his wife were exiled to unoccupied France in early 1943.

Chapter 11

Catholics During the Occupation

In the calamity that had befallen France, the Churches, though entirely blameless for what had happened, nonetheless had to shoulder a heavy burden. In accordance with established law, the men of peace set aside robe and cassock to join their parishioners in the national effort. Whether Catholic, Protestant or Jew, all Ministers of military age were mobilised. The Catholics being the most numerous, as one would expect for a country known as *la fille ainée de l'Eglise*[41] and still fundamentally faithful to Rome, the burden fell heaviest on them. Even the *"Pères Blancs"*[42] of the African Missions, important auxiliaries of the church administration as they were, had to join up. They went off, uncomplainingly, in 1939 as they had in 1914. With the surrender, most of the younger priests were taken to Germany as prisoners, leaving the churches depleted. The Germans kept the priests close prisoners, all but the few who, thanks to the efforts of Scapini, the Prisoners' Ambassador, were released as Army Red Cross Auxiliaries.

In occupied France, the Germans took over seminaries, schools, convents, monasteries, parish halls and even playing fields. On occasion the sanctity of the cloister was violated. In contrast with military establishments, many of the ecclesiastical buildings were modern and clean, and therefore the more coveted. Yet somehow, after the Armistice, posts were filled, classes improvised, schools reopened, the good word preached from pulpits as of yore.

Jack-booted crop-headed German priests stalked into churches, exhibiting credentials. The masses they said were sometimes served by the curés themselves, giving examples of humility, but even on

41. The elder daughter of the church.
42. White Fathers.

the plane of Christian solidarity the Teuton remained callous. They seized upon the little Pompeyan *bijou* that was the Empress Eugénie's Chapel in Biarritz and reserved it for themselves. One day the Curé of Sainte Eugénie, Biarritz's largest Parish Church, received notice that the Germans required the building on a certain Sunday at 10 a.m. That was the normal time for Sunday High Mass. However, services were re-organised to accommodate the request. At five minutes to ten the Germans marched up. The Commanding Officer halted his men outside the Church and went in. The officiating priest was still at the alter finishing mass and the congregation was getting ready to depart. The German Officer strode right up to the steps of the altar where the priest was kneeling, tapped him on the shoulder and pointed to his watch. The priest paid no attention, finished his prayers with the officer standing over him and then walked to the sacristy, with the German officer still at his side. The priest quietly pointed to the clock which showed one minute to ten.

At Saint Charles, another Biarritz Church, the Curé was in the pulpit giving his sermon. The altar was of course vacant whilst the priest was in the pulpit. Slipping behind the priest's back, literally and figuratively, a German Chaplain who had been saying mass at a side altar, entered the sacristy door, mounted the altar steps, opened the Tabernacle and proceeded to administer Holy Communion to a German soldier who had come to kneel at the foot of the altar. The priest, in the midst of his sermon, was astonished to see the congregation rise from their seats and go down on their knees in reverence when the Holy Presence was exposed, but once aware of what was taking place, he interrupted his sermon, turned and knelt.

If studied insult to the two Curés had been intended, it could hardly have been better planned to humiliate them and their congregations. However, these instances do not appear to have been intentional but merely amounted to spontaneous display of the German mentality. In contrast, the natural French turn of mind was displayed when a preacher, discoursing on *les malheurs de la France*,[43] described the country as being, like Christ Himself, crucified between two thieves. This was happening in the summer of 1940 when Mussolini's stab-in-the-back rankled fresh and deep.

Marshal Pétain was quick to lift the ban on members of the Religious Orders as teachers. He would even have assimilated the clergy as civil servants and given them salaries. Wisely, they preferred to remain independent while accepting financial support for their colleges as well as the extension of the benefit of scholarships.

The German-supporting Paris press soon began to denounce the religious of all categories as amongst the worst enemies of the Government. It was outrageous and preposterous, clamoured *Je Suis Partout*, that the clergy should pretend to ignore that it was the German victory which had made possible the benefits conferred and which also enabled them to be continued, for should England win, all these benefits would disappear. The paper went on to say: "the clergy, whether secular or regular, is poisoned by democracy, imbued with the spirit of the *Vicaire Savoyard* to the point that one saw French Catholics upholding the cause of the wandering Jew, the fanatical Anglo-Saxon Protestant and the godless Russian, against their German, Italian, Hungarian, Croat and Spanish co-religionists".

To the above outburst the *Bulletin Diocésain*, organ of the Basque Clergy, replied: "Such ill temper calls neither for lengthy commentary nor violent rejoinder. Good Frenchmen have other things to do than quarrel amongst themselves. It has always been an honour for the clergy to be criticized by both Right and Left; proof that it keeps the middle course." Marshal Pétain, at Pau, paid homage to the priests of France: "That honour suffices; they are decided to be ever worthy of it; they possess an ideal and dabble not in ideologies; they have leaders; their Bishops, models of loyalty and it is to them that they look for guidance along the straight path laid down by the Assembly of Cardinals and Archbishops, never to be confounded with the tortuous lanes of politics".

43. Misfortunes.

The spontaneity and vigour shown by a small provincial newspaper in taking up the challenge thrown down by a powerful Parisian publication indicates the spirit of independence and patriotic vigilance maintained by the French priests. Though disciplined and respectful of authority, few of them became zealous collaborationists, apart from the notorious case of Cardinal Baudrillart, Rector of the Catholic University of Paris. Too great was their sense of dignity. Moreover, the Germans cut the grass under their own feet by censoring ecclesiastical publications and going so far as to forbid reproduction of Vatican broadcasts and even passages of Encyclicals. What French Priest could consent to that? Their sensitivities as men, as priests and as patriots enabled them to distinguish between right and wrong, to deplore the triumph of violence and to condemn the abuse of power.

A tall ascetic figure in brown habit (deported later to Germany with his Abbot) wrings his hands, exclaiming in an agony of pent-up feeling: *"Ah, nous avons perdu jusqu'à l'honneur"*.[44] The bright sunlight of July 1940 illumined the scene as the solitary figure, ignoring for once the magnificent views stretching out from the gate of his monastery, paced, distraught, the avenue of ancient trees crowning a glorious foothill in the Pyrenees. Beyond anxiety for the fate of absent novices and beyond worries of the prospect of eviction, the Prior's thoughts flew to the devastating moral import of the Armistice.

A gentler, though no less significant, memory is that of a little Dominican Sister in her white robe and black cloak passionately deploring rough words flung at an old Jew when attacks on the long-persecuted race began again.

In every circumstance the position held by the Catholic Church in France places it in the forefront when crises befall. In the sincere effort of reconstruction undertaken for France's recovery by Marshal Pétain, in which the restoration of moral values was as imperative as material rebuilding, the clergy, conscious of its responsibilities, stood in the front rank.

44. We have lost our very honour.

While zealously exercising its influence on the side of law and order, the French clergy nonetheless maintained its independence of judgement and exercised criticism whenever it felt bound to do so. When, in June 1942, the Minister of Education, Abel Bonnard, proposed that collective promises of obedience to the Marshal's régime should be made by school children in the presence of a State Commissioner, ecclesiastical authorities at once protested, recalling the teachings of Pius XI that "an oath is always an act of religion". In these circumstances, the ecclesiastical warning went on, it is not permissible for children to become perjurers.

On the other hand, the clergy, seconded by the Religious Orders, became the leaders of useful effort, extending the scope of charitable institutions to meet the growing misery and ceaselessly teaching the necessity for constancy, self-reliance and hard work.

"How quickly the days pass, even unhappy days", reflected an ecclesiastical writer in June 1941, adding: "The days are a web in a nightmare of rapid, horrible visions in which we take a hand, though often unconsciously. We are too close-up to judge, understand or distinguish. We swim along half-drowned. So, reflex action takes the place of reasoned conduct. Complaints, criticism, bile are our daily pittance, coarse bread at which we nonetheless snatch with delight. The event of a year ago should have moved us to a useful conversion, namely an act of humility. We soon, however, found scapegoats, omitting ourselves naturally enough. We who so rarely forget ourselves, have neglected to measure our own submission, our own cowardliness, in the effort to discover faults which were ours in equal degree. Or else we gave proof of excessive modesty – a very general confession sufficed to set our conscience at rest. *Nostra culpa* substituted for *mea culpa*; anonymous contrition. Is it to be wondered the proclivity to sin continued?

"The conversion our humility should have heralded ought to have borne fruit in action. Because to collect one's thoughts is not in itself a virtue unless as a prelude to new departures and saving endeavour. In fact, we did at first applaud the proposed programme of work and restoration, exclaiming our approval in response to the call for sacrifice. However, we promptly let the spirit of ease recapture us. Rather than settle down to hard and applied labour, we sought and found excuses – the times were uncertain. What was the good of starting since nothing would last? The prospects of a fresh disaster – hands fell at the thought of disasters imminent. Or else – oh contradiction! – an artless fate in miracles appeared. Opportunism allied to pessimism – *a Deus ex machina* would surely arise someday to chase away the nightmare. Or else we became afflicted with a new and very sharp sense of honour – all our reserve of courage and pride breaking down under a flood of recrimination and criticism.

"There was, of course, the anguish arising from the most terrible problem of all – how to get on with everyday life. How to prepare for the future while the present offered nothing but hunger and misery. Enough energy remained, however, to run after the least sign of profit, to jump at any opportunity of filling one's pockets, for since Pharaonic times lean days have provided opportunities to become rich. Thus, little by little we wasted our chances of conversion. Some never budged from the mud in which they delight to wallow; others somehow found an easy and pleasant life; and yet others locked themselves up in a tower, there to weep, rave or curse.

"Must we despair? Only if the best among us continue refusing to understand that the hour for action, and not for weeping and alarm, has sounded. Action is always possible. It remains for each of us, according to the difficulties with which one is faced, to make necessary adjustments and adaptations, to toil in silence, tirelessly and without respite. Effort is the road to success. And, all said and done, is not faith in the future a victory in itself?" So wrote a man, a strong-hearted patriot, in an obscure diocesan sheet. Like most of the *petit curés*[45] of France, he came from the people, from sound stock.

The persecution to which the Jews were subjected appalled the conscience of the French clergy. In occupied France, where the Germans

45. Humble parish priests.

could impose their will and martial law was in force, no collective action could be taken although many were the religious who, in common with others, held out helping hands to the persecuted and were, in consequence, punished by the Germans.

In unoccupied France it was another matter, for a period at least. Cardinal Gerlier, primate of Gaul at Lyons, and the Archbishop of Toulouse, were amongst the first to publicly protest against the measures breaking up Jewish families, sending the men to one camp, the women to another, and the children to reformatories. While ready to support constitutional authority to the full and stand behind Marshal Pétain in his sincere efforts to reform, the Church of France felt bound to disapprove the odious measures violating the rights of man and running contrary to the teachings of Christ, as well as to the feelings of the French people. "If the right of sanctuary existed today as yore" proclaimed the Archbishop of Toulouse, "I would open my churches to the Jews".

In the summer of 1942 the *Bulletin Diocésain* of Bayonne, published under German occupation, declared unflinchingly: "The times in which we live favour heroic actions and exploits of all sorts but also every kind of excess and injustice. Under the pretext of the new order and of revolution, the sorriest enterprises of hate and passion are admitted, justified and even praised. Against such debauchery it becomes the duty of all men of heart to proclaim the just principles of human and Christian fraternity ..... the human person is inviolable and sacred...." The Germans promptly forbade publication of the *Bulletin* but the torch was nonetheless kept alight in every presbytery of the *Pays Basque.* The Bishop of Bayonne preserved such an uncompromising attitude towards the Germans that they put a guard over him. He died a recluse in his own palace.

An address delivered by Léon Bérard, Ambassador to the Vatican, to the French Ecclesiastical Colony in Rome, gives the measure of the importance attached by Marshal Pétain to securing the support of the clergy, at home and abroad. Bérard, a distinguished Senator, had fulfilled the delicate mission of re-establishing France's relations with General

Franco in 1939, and Marshal Pétain, while Ambassador at Burgos, had learnt to appreciate the solid diplomatic gifts of his predecessor. In his Vatican address M Bérard said: "Nothing shows more clearly the source and trend of the policies of our Chief than the resistance with which they are met. The Marshal does not subordinate the future of our country to the fickleness of fortune nor to the events which we would not have created but whose supposed virtue would be such as to efface our misfortunes without our having to question their origin. He believes that, in any case, a profound reform of our institutions and customs is necessary, not only by common consent of all Frenchmen but with the general and disciplined support of each one of us. According to the Marshal's views, the French Renaissance he desires must derive its source, energy and progress from the substance of the Nation. In whatever walk of life they happen to work, all are invited to participate in this Renaissance by giving professional activity its place of honour once more and integrating it with the Nation's recovery. The individual support solicited should be all the more readily forthcoming and the more efficacious because it is sought in the natural domain of family, soil, province and calling. In this new France, liberty will be found in hierarchies and unity. It is by picking up the threads of an historic experience that France would prepare for the new modalities and changes the world must expect. There will be no need for France to renounce her character when taking her place in the new community of peoples. It would indeed be a false interpretation of the acts and words of the Head of State and of his Government to imagine that they would ever sacrifice the spiritual autonomy, the moral identity as it were, of *La Patrie.* What sort of contribution could the world expect from a France prepared to forsake its origins?

"As this great work goes forward, in the circumstances and amidst the tremendous difficulties we all know, the most pressing duty for all Frenchman may be summed up in a simple but necessary order, at one and the same time a precept for the individual and a watchword for the citizen: Union, discipline, truce to idle discussion, to radical pronouncements on matters beyond one's knowledge, to auguries for the future of the world, or even of France, based on fragile conjecture; simpler still to place trust in our leaders and follow the advice of theologians who warn us against the demons of the spirit ready to pounce on and exploit man's ancient propensity towards pride and credulity, so aptly called *le sens propre.*

"Everything warns us to beware. It has been above all by union and unity that France has risen time and again from the depths. Let us recall the most miraculous episode in our history: the mission of Jeanne d'Arc. The saint of Lorraine, invested with the gift of commanding soldiers and winning battles, did not begin her task by raising armies and seeking the enemy. Her first care, the first manifestation of her vocation, was to make Frenchmen understand that salvation depended on certain rules of conduct. If they wished to be delivered they must put aside their quarrels by rallying to the Chief and to the political power designated by the laws of the Kingdom.

"The miraculous action of Jeanne followed the path of reason. The Church, in her own domain and exercising her attributions, recognised in the life and actions of Jeanne a supernatural virtue and made a saint of the girl who, though ignorant of all learning, had acted along the true lines followed by the builders of French unity.

"Let us admit that today the teachings of *la bonne Lorraine* have lost nothing of their value. The more uncertain our fate may seem, together with the fate of the world menaced by so many perils, the more we should be ready to understand, as she did, the precondition for salvation. Let us unite, avoiding every occasion not only of dissidence but of disagreement among Frenchmen. Whatever the future may reserve, unity is the only course which will not bring us deception or disappointment. An end to vain disputes as the means of repairing our misfortunes! There is no military defeat from which a people like ours cannot arise if only we remain faithful to our memories and ready to employ our talent and resources. Irremediable disaster can only come from ourselves. It would happen only the day when, owing to our divisions or to one of those public quarrels so ferocious and unending because the questions involved lay beyond our reach, we would give the world the feeling that we had lost our sense of destiny. The Marshal has asked us to partake of his great expectations. We shall not send our hopes into exile. They will remain with his on the soil he has saved twice".

Ambassadors always find a ready way to the hearts of expatriates by the mere mention of their absent homeland. One can imagine therefore the force of M. Bérard's address in the unhappy circumstances of its delivery, two years after the national collapse, but one doubts if he succeeded in his purpose on this occasion. Tears may well have dropped on many a *soutane* during the eloquent oration, but trained minds will have picked out the sophisms and contradictions in the discourse. Back in the quiet peace of their colleges, monasteries and convents, in the whitewashed rooms adorned only by a crucifix, where the plans for the conversion of sinners are constantly in progress, when priests and missionaries from *la douce France* ask themselves 'whence came the threat to France and her Empire, from the Allies or the Axis?', the answer must have come echoing down the broad new avenues and tortuous old streets of the Eternal City with the cries "Nice! Corsica! Tunis! *Duce, Duce, Duce*"

In the peaceful watches of the night, passages of Monsieur M. Bérard's eloquence may flit across wakeful minds, especially the invitation to remain faithful to old memories. What can be more vivid to any Frenchmen than the thought of Germany's constantly recurring aggressions. Three times in a century is too much. Yes, in truth, *"si seulement il reste fidèle à ses souvenirs"*,[46] the French people will rise again. *Por la Boca muere el pez* (by his mouth the fish dies) says the strange Castilian proverb. So, M. Bérard, in eight words inspired by instinctive patriotism, when heart overcame mind, uncovered himself.

In their prayers to Saint Joan, young seminarists in Rome may well ponder whether the girl-martyr, if she returned in her shining armour, would enlist under the betrayed Marseillaise at Vichy or with General de Gaulle and his Marche Lorraine? Faithful to their mission, French

46. If only he remains faithful to his memories.

priests laboured unceasingly in the Oflags and Stalags of Germany and in all formations where there were Frenchmen. Despite his venerable age, Monsignor de Nayol went to Russia so that the French Legionaries should have a Chaplain. The Abbé Pierrat, a Colonel while fighting proceeded in 1939 – 40, resumed his cassock after the Armistice and subsequently became Chaplain to the First Air Regiment in North Africa.

Of course, when the *Maquisards* took to the hills, priests followed them. Near Le Puy, where the Jesuits have a college, the Germans shot and flung into a common grave a number of Frenchmen. Working at night and with considerable risk, young Jesuits dug up the corpses, marked each one and established a record with all objects that might serve to identify the deceased. If they could do nothing for the dead, at least they might help to relieve the anxiety of relatives and spare long agonies of uncertainty.

So, in all spheres and circumstances, French priests conceived and practised the duty of charity.

If, during the period of revival, the French people were to listen more to the advice given by the devoted parish priests, the Nation would benefit and Frenchmen would find in reconciliation the road to unity. General de Gaulle found the portals of Nôtre Dame de Paris wide open to him.

Chapter 12

Wine, Women and Tobacco

Wine, fashions and tobacco count as three of the most precious amongst French products. Along with everything else, all three were hit hard by war conditions, which it was beyond the power of the Vichy Government to remedy. Nevertheless, all three maintained their importance and were almost the only sectors of French industry that remained completely in French hands throughout the Occupation. Germans drank less of the wine than might be supposed, influenced the fashions not at all, and smoked little of the "Caporal"[47] which irritated their throats.

Before the war, France produced half the wine of Europe and three sevenths of world output. Out of forty million Frenchmen, seven million, together with their families, lived by wine; all forty million drank it to the tune of three litres per week per head of population.

In 1939–40 the crop was 100 million hectolitres, which, owing to lack of labour, sulphate and manures, fell to 78 million in 40–41; 58 million in 41–42 and 47 million in 42–43. Algeria and Tunisia, whence had been shipped respectively 16 and 1 million hectolitres of wine to France in 1938, ceased to contribute at all in 1942.

The French wine industry had experienced great crises in the past. Mildew in 1874–5 and phylloxera in 1878–90 both did immense harm. But then, and also during 1914–18, all difficulties had been overcome without recourse to rationing or any serious limitation of consumption. This was because professionals were left in charge whereas, under the Vichy régime, functionaries of all ilk were let loose. These gentlemen fixed prices before ascertaining the importance of the crop, imposed impracticable regulations and did everything necessary to rouse the

47. A common brand of tobacco.

opposition of wine growers as well as to ruin them. They maintained the pre-war policy of reducing production, so that in the years 1939 -43, in the Hérault region alone, some 90,000 acres of vines were eliminated. In this manner, during three years of increasing demand and dire national necessity, some 12% of France's vineyards were destroyed.

Wine is obviously an immensely important part of everyday life in France. So when early in 1941 *vin ordinaire*, that is to say household wine sold on draught, disappeared from the market and the price of bottled wine, or as the French call it *vin de marque*, soared, there were howls of complaint. After some months, the Government decided to distribute a general wine ration of one litre per week. This is one third of what Frenchmen were used to drinking, but the deprivation was tempered by a more generous ration for workers, according to the strenuousness of their trade: smiths, engine drivers, fishermen and coal miners got double rations. It became a grievance with the peasants and gardeners that they were never classed as *travailleurs de force*,[48] but there was a special allowance for harvesters working in the fields. Wine growers were allowed to keep a portion of their crop for consumption or private sale. It was not long before wine growers of the South and farmers of the Centre and North got together and found a way of helping each other in getting around the law. This was done, perfectly correctly, by each party exchanging acreages of their lands with the other, the farmer figuring as proprietor of a vineyard and vice versa. In this manner, the farmer was able to invoke privileges granted under the law only to the wine growers. He thus obtained wine independently of rationing while the growers insured themselves winter supplies of potatoes and carrots as well as eggs, poultry and pigs. By these arrangements, the French spirit asserted itself once more while the Administration went its way and, in theory, continued to exercise strict control.

The height of ridicule in these regulations was reached when it became impossible for a person sitting down in a restaurant in Béziers

48. Labourers.

– a district which produces, annually, as much wine as the entire population of Germany, Greece or Bulgaria – to buy a glass of *vin ordinaire*. With gallons of it in every cellar in town, restaurant owners were obliged to declare *"il n'y en a pas, Monsieur"* and to offer v*in controlé* at 90 Francs per bottle. On the other hand, a Frenchman will always be happy to pay for wine, even a high price for a good wine. Thus, it came about that the restrictions played directly into the hands of the black market. Wine merchants made fortunes, literally thrust upon them by circumstance. Thousands of new "brands" appeared since it was sufficient to supply a name, label and cap to a bottle in order to obtain a licence to sell it as *vin controlé,* a vintage hitherto unclassified. Small growers, who had been working family presses from father to son for centuries, selling their wine locally or to a small circle of customers, suddenly found that, quite legally, they could obtain 100 to 150 times the former price. This profiteering went on quite openly and without shame. One well-known firm claimed to have made a profit of 1 billion francs. The war wine boom will supply an interesting chapter to post-war stories.

According to Léon Douarche, an authority on French viticulture and from whom the foregoing figures are quoted, France's total export trade in wines in 1938 was valued at 800 million francs, of which 320 millions were champagne and 180 Bordeaux – mere footling figures compared to the value of the home market during the war years. The Bordeaux trade was killed by the blockade but the Champagne crops were bought by the Germans for Central and Northern Europe. Despite reports that German trenches at Stalingrad were full of Cognac bottles, growers from there were saying quite categorically that there would be plenty for the Americans to drink when they disembarked. The sole virtue of the "ration" wine was that it remained relatively cheap, averaging about 10 francs per litre. Once a year, a tumbler full of rum or brandy was issued, a meagre portion "to ward off winter chills" as the ill-advised but would-be paternalistic Government would have it.

Government policy, so generous to the wine merchants, proved equally bountiful for the Paris dressmakers, whilst enraging all the rest.

Those responsible for framing the early dress-rationing regulations stated that *"l'honneur du chic français"* demanded that no such grubby insult as the issuing of coupons should be imposed on the *grands couturiers.*[49] On the other hand, to allow even one business to evade the law was to open up dire possibilities of abuse, as well as to risk accusations of injustice. Nonetheless, the gallant gentlemen at the head of the new National Revolution decided that not one firm but 40 should be allowed the privilege of selling anything they wanted to in the way of clothes – no inspectors, no questions for these aristocrats of the fashion business. What an opportunity for them! Up went prices in this industry just as in the branded-wines trade, so that by 1944, 30,000 francs for a tailor-made suit in woollen material, acquired most likely at a couple of 100 francs per yard – was no out-of-the-way figure. Like painters and sculptors, these privileged dressmakers were in a position to command any price they could get and there always seemed to be plenty of rich people prepared to pay the price. One small formality was required of them, however – that of procuring a purchaser's card. To secure this, they were asked to subscribe 200 francs towards the Prisoners' Fund and donate one kilogram of wool to a war charity. Thus, a pleasant touch of patronage was given to these transactions. Formerly, grand ladies would drop a franc to the hand of a beggar at the door but now they had to pay 1200 Fr on the black market for the kilogram of wool. Despite this gesture, revolutionary stalwarts roundly denounced the system which they averred led to monstrous abuse and was contrary to the true interests of French elegance. Certainly, the wholesale dressmaking firms and countless private workers were at a serious disadvantage because the pick of new material was supplied preferentially to the *maisons dérogées.*[50] These privileged firms, being in a position to recover their costs from their customers, were able to purchase freely on the black market all manner of threads, linings and the many accessories which become more difficult to obtain than material. Thus, the inevitable tendency was to encourage profiteering,

49. Great fashion houses.
50. Derogated firms.

that ominous cloud looming ever blacker over the horizon of the poor, struggling French.

Dame Fashion continued to exercise her time-honoured privilege of tyranny, decreeing big hats and voluminous skirts while materials becoming ever scarcer. There was a touch of defiance towards the Occupying Power when Cossack hats and coats appeared when the German Army retreated from Stalingrad and German propagandists and their French collaborators denounced evermore loudly the "*Bolshevist Menace.*" On the other hand, adorable little cycling costumes, eminently practical, were devised for a world reduced from motor car to *vélo. The Parisienne* never lost her chic. Her struggle – and it was a real one – was just one way among others of keeping the tricolour flying. Everybody knows the *article de Paris* trade which is accessory to, and in a sense tributary of, the *Modes*,[51] and even more than it, a luxury industry. To what sore straights was it reduced when leather, gold, silver, crystal, varnishes and silks vanished! It never, however, quite gave up the ghost although, by force of circumstance, it had to direct its efforts into new channels, catering for available, if undesirable, customers, namely the Germans, both soldiers and civilians, who frequented the shopping streets, ready to purchase. They were not *connaisseurs* and it was easy to palm-off second-rate goods. It would not be right to judge the Parisian artisan's craft when he worked "to live", though he certainly exercised much ingenuity in devising new articles and employing ersatz materials. For old customers he continued to produce charming, expensive trifles as of yore so that at New Year *Monsieur* might offer to *Madame* perchance a little, leakproof, silver *repoussé*[52] casket into which to pop the bag of wet leaves she fished out of the emptied teapot at the Café de la Paix, to eke out next morning's breakfast. For *Madame* to present *Monsieur* with a little fancy box, inspired by ancient snuff, powder or patch-boxes in which to collect his cigarette ends or cigar stubs. Economy became the order of the day after 1940, even in the most aristocratic circles of Paris and left little room for false shame.

51. Fashions.
52. Hand-embossed.

As an administrative machine the Vichy Government made a poor show in its handling of the smoking issue. Inequalities were created, abuses allowed and a much-needed source of revenue for the state forfeited. At first, the rule was that tobacco cards were to be distributed solely to men who could prove that they were smokers. Many women were confirmed smokers but the Government ignored them completely. This sweeping challenge to French gallantry was taken up immediately. Every man in the country, whatever his private feelings towards Dame Nicotine, immediately declared himself an ardent worshipper at her shrine and claimed his right to the 120 cigarettes, or three packets of piped tobacco, or three cigars, fixed at first as the National monthly ration. It wasn't much but it was shared with the fair sex and no one can say that any French woman smoked the less because of the washouts at Vichy.

Before the war, "blue gauloises"[53] cigarettes and "grey" tobacco (so called from the colour of the wrappers) made up 80% of consumption. This popular mixture, better known as *Caporal*, was composed of 50% French grown tobacco, 20% American, 20% Algerian and 10% mixed origin. At one fell swoop, therefore, France had to fall back on home production. When Algeria was lost, the above meagre ration was reduced to 80 cigarettes, 20 cigars or 2 packets of piped tobacco, per month.

Although both the French climate and soil were propitious to tobacco-growing, it was not until the fourth year of the war that any official effort was made to extend cultivation. Instead, the Government factories began experimenting with ersatz products such as the leaf of the Jerusalem artichoke. These mixtures were so resolutely disliked by smokers that the attempt was abandoned.

Meanwhile, private initiatives took over in defiance of State monopoly, so that by 1942 there was hardly a garden or field without some tobacco plants. Home-curing of the leaf was not up to scratch at first but improved with the passage of time. Pipe-smokers were quite content

53. Popular cigarette brand.

with the strong, black, home-grown product and thus thousands of tobacco cards went into the black market. The Government monopoly accepted defeat and made the best of a bad job by extending cultivation to new regions where farmers were allowed to plant whole fields of tobacco on the basis of payment by the State, in money or in kind. If the monopoly had forestalled private initiative by extending cultivation earlier, it might have saved the situation by keeping production apace with demand thus maintaining its privileged position and securing greatly increased revenue. Now it will be very difficult to stamp out private cultivation, as both experience and skill have been built up. The black market in tobacco, on the other hand, will most likely be killed off when prices go back down to normal.

In the years following 1940 barmen all over the country would eagerly pay 100 francs for a packet of 20 cigarettes, sold by the Government monopoly for 12 francs, and resell them at 150 francs. Secondary tobacco, used for inferior cigarettes, the little grey *(petit gris),* popular in normal times, fetched anything up to 1,500 francs per kilogram. In large towns, especially in Paris, "Lucky Strikes" and "Camels" never quite disappeared and were sold for fabulous prices. Sometimes they were smoked in a holder, passed along the bar counter at 2 francs a whiff – a flash of snobbery on the part of the *"Zazous"*, as the idle youth came to be called. The prison camps in France seem to have been the main supply points of Virginian tobacco, especially after the internment of Americans. A well-known American barman in Paris, who spent a fortnight at Compiègne, came away with a parcel representing a fortune and with which he was able to restock his establishment.

Not least in this whole saga, as the franc slumped, tobacco, which always had a rising market and was so much more easily handled than packets of grease or butter, became a ready means of exchange.

Chapter 13

If?

One of the questions which tortured Frenchmen during the long months of moral and physical distress was whether it would not have been better for the Government to have endeavoured to reach Algeria under protection of the Fleet and continue the struggle from there or elsewhere in the French Empire.

The hopes that divided the leaders during those few fateful hours at Bordeaux in 1940 when the project actually lay in the balance, returned, long after it had been firmly turned down by Marshal Pétain, to trouble the minds of citizens when any possibility of its happening had long vanished and nothing remained but a chimera decked with the glamour of what might have been.

Like many great decisions in history, Marshal Pétain's determination to remain in France at all costs seems destined to be one of those disputed acts of leadership that must remain so until history, at some distant date, pronounces with clear-sighted judgement. Contemporaries are too close to the tremendous event, too swayed by passion, too subject to inferences of the moment, to be able to decide. Nor is the ordinary mortal, bereft of elements of appreciation, in a position to say wherein or wherenot lay the national good.

During the few hours while preparations for emigration were proceeding, that is to say while the die-hards in Paul Reynaud's cabinet, with Mandel of Clemenceau memory at their head, were embarking at Le Verdon on the Massilia and President Lebrun's chauffeur was studying his map for the shortest road to Port Vendres, the chief as well as the cheapest argument against the exodus was the cry *"on n'emporte pas la Patrie à la semelle de ses souliers"*.[54] Danton's famous cry, in equally

54. One doesn't walk off with the Fatherland.

critical circumstances, amounted to an instinctive expression for some, though for others was merely an echo of defeatism. The cry, however, embodied the essence of the theme as the matter depended on what Frenchmen accepted as the definition of *La Patrie.*

Ask a hundred Frenchmen to define *La Patrie* and ninety-nine will reply in simple astonishment that you should have put such a question – *"mais la Patrie, c'est la France"*. Undoubtedly the popularity of Pétain's decision to remain was due to the superficial identity, in the mind of the average Frenchman, of *La Patrie* and *La France.* Any deeper spiritual conception of nation and empire was, for now, submerged. It may well also be that, in the mind of the aged Marshal himself, a vision of the humble farm in Artois, where he was born 84 years previously, figured prominently at that supreme moment and overshadowed considerations of statesmanship.

However this may be, the danger to France subsequently became apparent as suffering increased and the hard lessons of circumstance forced Frenchmen to realise, by remaining, that *le Gouvernment du Maréchal* had forfeited all independence worthy of the name and sold the Nation into spiritual as well as material bondage. Bound hand and foot by the outrageous economic conditions of the Armistice (accepted, doubtless, in the belief that England would succumb and the war would be over in a few months), the Vichy Government soon found itself in a sorry and humiliating state. For nearly two years thereafter, the Marshal struggled to preserve the essence of *"l'Armistice dans L'honneur"* he had conceived.

Could the Government have got away in 1940? Could it have maintained itself in North Africa once there? What would have happened in France in the meantime? What course would the war have taken? These questions, idle as they had become, nevertheless returned to inspire doubts as crisis succeeded crisis at Vichy and the general situation in France continued to deteriorate.

Doubtless the Ministers might have departed in a squadron of planes or in a single ship but to transport a substantial body of civil servants and, above all, the armed forces, a large amount of merchant tonnage and some weeks' preparation would have been necessary.

Such an operation, for which only three ports of any consequence remained, namely Bordeaux, Marseilles and Port Vendres, as well as the Toulon Arsenal, would have required forward planning, if only to assemble the departing mass and requisite ships. No such plan existed. The eventuality had never even been remotely envisaged by the Government or its General Staff. Moreover, at the time it was mooted, the Germans had so effectively broken French resistance that they had been able to march in a few days, practically unopposed, from Paris to Lyon and to the Swiss frontier. Established in the Rhone Valley, the Panzers were in a position to bypass the Massif Central and could have thrust forward to Marseilles in a few hours on the first sign that the Government and the remains of the Army were endeavouring to embark. Bordeaux was equally within striking distance of the German positions near Orléans and Tours. Nor were the French forces at the disposal of General Weygand after the fall of Paris in any way adequate to cover embarkation points, especially such widely divergent ones as Bordeaux and Marseilles. The former would have had to have been abandoned and everything staked on establishing a barrier for a last stand in the Rhone Valley.

In such hasty flight, a few hundred officials and some thousands of troops carrying a modicum of equipment, might have got away. France's scrappy aviation might have flown off but could not have taken with it any of the magnificent modern equipment the air factories had recently received from America. The Fleet would have sailed but the last French arsenal, Toulon, would have been lost. In North and West Africa, with Bizerta, Algiers, Mers el Kébir, Casablanca and Dakar, the Navy disposed of fine bases, but they could only have given harbourage because, for repairs and munitionment, the Fleet relied on its home arsenals. Nor did Algeria have any industrial organisation to fall back on or that could have served as a nucleus for expansion. All resources to carry on would have had to have been imported urgently; arms, equipment, clothing and supplies. Such dependence on foreign help seemed not only preposterously impractical to the logical mind but was, moreover, insurmountably galling to French pride.

The last-minute offer made by the British Government for common citizenship met with no response from France. It is doubtful if the people on the whole ever realised what it implied. For success, such proposals need to be put forward as further progress over a long period of international intimacy, not sprung in emergency as if obeying a counsel of despair. Coming as a result of years of exchange between French and English school children, and their families, on the basis of mutual visits and a certain co-ordination of education, both secondary and academic, as well as the careful fostering of an intimacy of ideals which undoubtedly already existed, such an offer might have bridged the great emergency that had arisen. Instead, the generosity of the proposal was lost in the turmoil of the moment and its meaning misunderstood. It even caused resentment.

In general, the majority of the leaders felt that a government, ready to emigrate, was doomed in advance, not only for the above reasons but also because of the disapproval of most Frenchmen. The French in France would have hastened to give themselves another government entitled, at least by territoriality, to call itself French. Pétain believed that there was still a chance (though disappearing hour by hour with the speed of the German advance) to save some of the homeland. That slight chance, coupled with abhorrence of the notion of flight, settled the question. In sum, the French Government of 1940 elected to desert France's allies rather than abandon French soil as distinct from the French cause, soul and Empire. A momentous decision which, as it turned out, jeopardised the Empire, wrought dissension among Frenchmen and brought destruction to the Fleet because the Nation, subconsciously, made a choice which was not the Marshal's.

Marshal Pétain, however, did not count himself in any way a Quisling. His presence at the head of the new *Ètat Français,* which so rapidly emerged from the old régime, helped by the astonishing suicidal vote of the National Assembly on 10 July 1940, undoubtedly prevented France from becoming immediately and utterly subservient to Germany. The subsequent disgrace of Laval in December that year affords proof of the old Marshal's independence of spirit. The Vichy Government was at first most certainly a great asset to England. Had it not been for the

Marshal's leadership, Laval would have had a free hand from the first to pick up the reigns of Government for the avowed purpose of bringing about rapidly and effectively the *"Renversement des Alliances"*[55] which the French defeatists, encouraged by their Berlin backers, never ceased to advocate as representing the true interests of France. Pétain put a spoke in that wheel all through the critical period of England's isolation and military impotence and so rendered a certain, if unintentional, service of inestimable value to the Allies.

The establishment of the *ligne de démarcation*[56] took some time, as did the setting up, in unoccupied France, of the Commissions to supervise demobilisation and to verify to German satisfaction that France was disarmed. For many months, considerable German forces were massed in France to meet emergencies. The possibility, however remote, of a diversion in his rear was, perhaps, a consideration of some weight in Hitler's mind to deter him from attempting the *attaque brusquée*[57] that might have proved fatal to a not-as-yet fully armed England.

Had the Bordeaux Government emigrated, German occupation of the whole of France would have become effective in a few days and all anxiety concerning French military power on the Continent would likewise have vanished. Furthermore, not only would the Axis grip in the Mediterranean have become immediately stronger with the possession of Toulon and Corsica, but, as master of the entire Pyrenean frontier, and not just a few miles of its Western end, Hitler's pressure on Spain would have been irresistible. General Franco would hardly have been able, as proved the case in October 1940 when he met the Führer at Hendaye, to keep his peace with Oliveira Salazar and head off his redoubtable visitor in another direction.

The presence in North Africa of the French Government would have acted like a magnet for the invasion of Spain, for which German troops immediately began to prepare on reaching the Bidassoa, hastily strengthening the frontier bridges and organising a *zone d'étapes*[58] for

55. Reversal of alliances.
56. Line dividing occupied from unoccupied France.
57. Sudden attack.
58. Staging point zone.

eighteen divisions around Bayonne. In this situation, with military action against the French remaining imperative, bases on the Spanish shore of the Mediterranean would have become necessary for the Reich. In all probability, therefore, long before the Luftwaffe appeared in Sardinia to threaten the Western approach to Alexandria, long before Gibraltar and Malta could have modernised their defences as they did, German bombers would have been down in the fields of Andalusia and Spanish Morocco. In this light the early fate of Gibraltar, Portugal and Spain hung on that fateful decision at Bordeaux which set in motion so many imponderable factors.

On the other hand it might be argued that, constituted around the considerable nucleus of military force already existing in North Africa, the remnants of France's metropolitan army, cooperating with the British forces in Egypt, plus the two Fleets, might conceivably have been able to expel the Italians quickly from Cyrenaica and Tripoli before the Germans had time to tighten their grip on Italy and the Balkans. For that, however, it would have been necessary to send out from England, immediately, large quantities of equipment, munitions, tanks, guns and aircraft. England did not have them to send. After her immense losses in Flanders, exhausted by her terrific initial effort to sustain France, before industrial war organisation had got into its stride, and with the danger of invasion becoming an imminent menace, all effort had to be concentrated on home defence. What indeed, could England have spared for overcrowded Algeria, become dependent on foreign supply even for food! Reality, the hard master, would have rendered impossible any defence of the new opportunity offered to Germany. A breathing space had become imperative for Great Britain. Paradoxically, Pétain's armistice provided it.

Deep run the waters of history in the making. Speculation and conjecture open fascinating vistas but they vanish like smoke once the die is cast. We are all playthings of Fate and what a grand game the old Jade had: France, the cloak tossed to the Teuton bull to engage his attention while Britain readied its defences.

Chapter 14

Marshal Pétain[59]

New Year, 1943

Philippe Pétain, Marshal of France, *Chef de l'Ètat Français* that supplanted the French Republic, one and indivisible, you have been treated harshly by circumstance since you issued that terrible pledge in June 1940. But you brought it on yourself when you claimed full responsibility and proudly left it to France and posterity to judge you.

That was nearly three years ago. At the time your prestige lifted countless hearts. In many a home, Frenchmen proudly hung your portrait and looked for guidance towards those fearless eyes and caesarean profile. Crowds collected as you made your way through towns and countryside and, as it is written of the Saints, "your presence brought comfort". You were still *le Grand Chef.* Those who believed that you had saved the soil of France, not once but twice, acknowledged you unconditionally as *le Père de la Patrie.* Then, in a gesture of generous abandon, you made that strange gift of your person to the Nation. The act was theatrical but the feeling behind it was understood and endeared you, the ancient warrior, still more to the people. It drew you to them and them to you, for better or worse, or so it appeared. Thus, you and all Frenchmen set forth into unchartered waters. Much was expected of you, perhaps too much, for strange as it may seem, those *anciens combattants*[60] believed to a man that the unquenchable spirit of Verdun, which they recognised personified in de Gaulle and his *Français libres*,[61] still inspired you. Had you not told them on 20 June 1940 that

59. This chapter was written in 1943.
60. Soldiers of 1914-18 war.
61. The Free French.

the fight remained the same, for France, her soil and her sons, and to add three days later: "Destiny lies in your courage and perseverance".

You had the Armistice Agreement in your pocket, based, as you said, on "honour between soldiers". You thought it would enable you to hold France and the Empire together, allowing you sufficient independence, in the reduced national territory behind the demarcation line, to lay the foundations for those reforms of which French society stood in dire need, as was generally acknowledged. The path was strewn with countless obstacles but, feeling yourself in possession of a clear line of conduct, you plunged ahead.

That was thirty long months ago. Now, what a contrast! Your clear line proved a snare and a delusion, for you were never allowed real independence to exercise initiative or to institute reforms other than base imitations of persecutory measures the French people repudiate and abhor. At most, you repaired some injustices such as the forbidding of ecclesiastical schools and laid the basis for a reorganization of agriculture and industry. You laid great store on the School of Chiefs, created in an old castle in the heart of France under the direction of a fine leader, General de la Porte du Theil, but he, like Weygand, was taken from you by the Germans. Your *Chantiers de la Jeunesse,* where all young men of twenty were obliged to give eight months' labour to the Nation, prospered until the Germans tried to make them recruiting centres for forced labour in the *Reich*. Thereafter, these youngsters, against your recommendation, preferred the *Maquis,* its hardships and perils, to high pay in Germany.

In a desperate attempt to escape the intolerable constraints imposed on you, your closest associates and most trusted counsellors have been driven to perjury and treason. Even before the fictitious border of your make-believe State was torn away, you had been forced to acknowledge that you were not free. In fact, you were already drifting with the tide when the clouds burst in Morocco and Algeria. So *"Le canon de Toulon"*, as it echoed from end to end of France, found you inaugurating an exhibition of Infant Art. To such futilities had von Runstedt's sudden visit reduced your prerogative as Chief of State. Your Young France continued its football while the Panzers rolled down to the shores of the Mediterranean. Likewise, your State broadcasts that night did not even mention your protest to Hitler's envoy. Football results, more football results, filled awkward pauses while you at Vichy exclaimed: "There is nothing left, nothing. It only remains for us to pray. Yet France is not a convent".

It did not much matter because all of France – including, perhaps, you yourself, privately – was listening to other voices relating events that thrilled the dullest heart and upon which depended the fate of France. The flood was rolling past your door, leaving you in your impotence high and dry on barren ground with, beside you, the man you yourself, just two years previously, had disgraced: Pierre Laval. To add insult to injury, your old comrade, General Weygand, was waylaid in one of your cars and carried off to Germany.

It must be maddening for you, Philippe Pétain, unless you are still sitting on the fence (and Laval with you) gaining what you can – years, months, weeks, hours for Time the avenger to come to the rescue. That, they point out, was the supreme purpose of the Armistice – to make a place for France where she could await the outcome of the war between her conqueror and her allies, while the war went forward. That events are not progressing in line with this hope is evident. Nevertheless, that has continued to be your game. Your proclaimed griefs against England, Laval's reproaches to America, his flattery of Hitler and Mussolini – all just part of the general flummery and creating the great smokescreen under which you cling to your trenches as tenaciously as you did at Verdun. Such is the belief, the extraordinary belief which is so widespread it must be recorded, however preposterous it may seem. Justification of duplicity, one asks? Is any necessary when dealing with Adolf Hitler, they reply.

But if so, what torture for you, brought up in the discipline of *droiture*[62] that is the soldier's tradition in the fair land of the Franks and who put faith in an Armistice *en tout bien et tout honneur.*[63]

62. Integrity
63. With honourable intentions.

You! now obliged to steep in an atmosphere of prevarication and vilipendium, actually to live in it the better to practise the letter of the dark Machiavellian precept of the end justifying the means, so that Hitler, the biter, be bitten; Hitler the cheater, be cheated!

Some would condone with the murmur "poor Pétain", only to strip you of your proudest prerogative as leader – your authority. Authority? Yes, that is where you have fallen down, for your countrymen have refused to follow you in certain directions, as part of their belief in others.

If you yourself have not intrigued you have certainly been surrounded by conspiracy from the first – conspiracy by Germans, conspiracy by the French. That nice little plot that was to have brought you back to Paris to receive a Judas kiss over the Duc de Reichstadt's[64] dust! You apparently saw through that one, and the unbending old lady, head of the Bonaparte clan, backed you up by refusing to allow the Germans into the ceremony. So the Nazis with their wreaths waited at the door where Admiral Darlan appeared, representing you, *Monsieur le Maréchal.* You did not think Paris worth a Mass, that is, a Paris with Germans in it. In this manner, despite the intrigue, the mortal remains of the son of the greatest soldier in French history came to rest beside those of his father. Thus, in December 1940, you dared give the Germans the cold shoulder and spurned Pierre Laval. The whole of France applauded your action. You entered the New Year high in the esteem of Frenchmen.

At Montoire, you had promised Hitler collaboration which you intended as just that, collaboration, not subservience. That is where you differed from Laval. The game was on. You had scored a point but you were far from through and were soon to learn it. The impulsive *Gascon,* Admiral Darlan, whom you had sent to Berchtesgaden on 23 December 1940, returned, having tried to please, but to no end. The enigmatic fellow who had clasped your hand at Montoire, without ever raising his eyes to yours, had made a terrible scene. Darlan brought back an ultimatum and you decided you must give ground. So Baudoin, Alibert,

64. Son of Napoleon.

Peyrouton and Flandin, that is those whom the slavish Paris Press designated as leaders of the so-called cabal of 13 December, departed and you consented to meet Laval in reconciliation on 18 January 1941. This was another of those fugitive railway station meetings that came to count so much in the destiny of France. The meeting at least saved appearances, with Laval refusing the post you offered him and *l'union des Français* being saved once again. In reality, divisions remained rife. On 10 February you reasserted yourself by promulgating Constitutional Act No.4, designating Admiral Darlan as your successor, the post he was to occupy until he decided that he too must switch sides. François Darlan became not only your successor-designate but your right hand, Commander-in-Chief of the combined armed forces of the *Ėtat Français,* head of the Foreign Office, Home Office and the Admiralty. In sum, your *homme de confiance,* all of which enabled him to declare in his representations to the Empire, when he went to Algiers, that he was the depository of your true thoughts and feelings.

But all that came much later. Long months of trial and strain lay ahead, during which, bit by bit, the German machine was grinding France to pieces before your eyes. Ah, that precious Armistice Agreement – what store do you set by it now? By December 1941, when you met Marshal Goering at Saint Florentin, you had a very different opinion on that matter. Hence the seven-page memorandum you fired at him. Once more it was Germans who wanted to get a proper sense of your commitment, this time on the eve of events in the Pacific. The Spanish Embassy again acted as go-between. Lequerica, the indolent, sleek-haired Maurist Deputy for Toledo, was now playing a role in the destinies of France! Marshal Goering began by requesting that you should show greater energy in defending France's African Empire, in particular the Tchad Territories on the flank of Rommel's prospective advance in the North. You replied that, in that case, it would be necessary for Germany to return French Officers, men and material, and you recalled how the same request had been made, to no avail, in the case of Syria. Regarding collaboration, you maintained this was impossible as long as the victor continued to throttle his victim. You then asked that your memorandum be read aloud, setting forth your grievances, France's grievances, since the signing of the Armistice and the meeting at Montoire. It made Goering exclaim: "But who are the victors, you or us"! He refused to transmit the document to his Fűhrer. You finished by pushing the document into his pocket.

When Goering complained that the yield from French agriculture was insufficient and the food supplies badly organised: "Give us back the 800,000 peasants you hold prisoner and return some of our rolling stock", you replied, protesting that as long as massive requisitions continued, France would have to starve. You also reminded Goering that France had already paid over greater sums than the total Germany had paid as a result of the 1914–18 war. Moreover, despite promises, Alsace-Lorraine had been ravished once more.

Alas, your show of spirit led to nothing, for the heart of the Teuton on the warpath knoweth no pity. With or without the Armistice, France's head is in the noose and ruthless Germany holds the rope. There is no way out of your dilemma, as fearsome today as on that fatal June morning in 1940. There can be no half-way house in a totalitarian war. It is neck or nothing. France must fight or succumb. Your great mistake is now apparent.

Frenchmen, even disarmed, refused to be enslaved. You misjudged, moreover, both the nature and vitality of the Empire. It had to live so Colony after Colony acknowledged the inspiring *Croix de Lorraine* on the upraised Tricolour. The undefeated Fleet might be neutralised by an order to anchor but not so the Empire. As a living force it continued to assert itself, and being a creation of the life-blood of France, it found the breath of liberty necessary for that. Your *Union des Français* is broken, or rather it never was. The spirit of France, incarnate in its Empire and in the Free French, spurn you while those Frenchmen who share your sorry fate, chained to the rock like Prometheus, pity you; all but the handful of traitors who would use you as their tool. Which wounds you the most, the scorn or the pity? That is your secret. We know only what you choose to reveal. In René Benjamin you have a faithful mouthpiece. He tells us of the "gravest confidences" you ever made to him. It was one day while you were taking an afternoon drive in the country around Vichy, shortly after Darlan's departure. It was a chilly day and, as you talked, you pulled the carriage rug well over your knees. In musing tones you said: "When I signed the Armistice, I gave my word. It only remains for me to keep it …….. but the French people in whose name I spoke have abandoned me. I hoped to govern by reciprocal confidence. It is never easy to govern. Some succeed by the use of force and maintain themselves in power by violence. But by confidence….!

"Frenchmen seem to think that 'deviousness' is something superior to honesty and they think I am with them in this, so intensely do they wish it so. But how could I conduct myself like this, I who tell schoolchildren never to cheat? The children seem to understand. I have had thousands of letters from them. But their parents? They remain tricksters at heart. Many others are weak, or neutral. How am I to harden them?"

Reneé Benjamin records that you added: "After all, this state of mind and lack of spirit is not wonderful but is perhaps better for the future of the world than vehement adhesion to imprudent mysticisms". You then added: "As regards myself, I shall never cheat. In war, ruse is perhaps permissible as part of the strategy but I am no longer a man of war. I have signed the Armistice. I shall keep my word no matter what". Then, after a deep breath: "I am not a prisoner of the enemy, I am a prisoner of my word". A long pause before adding: "Nor will I give in, because I have taken a second oath, this time to Frenchmen, not to abandon them in their time of trouble." Finally, in an even voice, you ended: "That is simple and it is final".

One wonders if, as you preside at Vichy, a subject of commiseration but still venerated by many Frenchmen and women, you find it as simple and final as that.

August 1944: In the glorious "month of abundance", as the French farmers call August and which, in this year of grace, is overflowing with the milk and honey of bountiful crops and the balm of spiritual elation, Marshal Pétain, now but a relic, is still at Vichy. Laval and his Government have fled, and with them around a thousand higher officials. Only the underlings remain, as well as a few members of the Diplomatic Corps. The old Marshal refused to follow Laval and the Ministers to Belfort. It was his last free decision. As he awaits his fate, he can meditate at leisure on the astonishing events of the past six months.

When bombings prior to the Allied Landings began devastating French towns far and wide, the Marshal went on his last tour – an errand of mercy to the newly devastated regions. From Rouen to Ėpinal, from Reims to Lyon, he was acclaimed everywhere he went. In Paris, the welcome was particularly warm. Boys and girls ran wildly along the *parvis*[65] at Notre Dame to catch a sight of his *képi*.[66] The Tricolour was hoisted for the first time in four years over the Hôtel de Ville. A soldier's *képi* and the Tricolour, French military emblems of which Parisians had been starved for interminable months. With their hearts uplifted at the prospect of coming Liberation, it was hardly surprising they were ready to cheer the old soldier, who will always be, whatever happens, part of the glory of France. Generosity goes with elation.

Were you duped, Marshal Pétain? If so, what do you think of the splendid gesture of the people of Paris rising to free themselves without awaiting the arrival of the Allies; of the thousands who have fought and died so that Paris might be free again, both from the Germans and from the defeatism of Vichy.

During those memorable days, a few short months before the triumph, on that same *parvis*, of the soldier you condemned to death because he had dared raise the Tricolour when you had lowered it, you issued one more of your messages to the French people – the last one allowed to be published – telling them that their "pretended liberation is the falsest of delusions". You uttered one more of those famous Pétainesque phrases adjuring Frenchmen always to maintain the correct attitude towards the invaders because "there can be no compromising with duty or the pledged word".

Finally, you invoked once again the defence of Europe by Germany, as paladin of Western Civilization. How could you believe that with

65. Open space in front of a church.
66. Military cap.

Germany's record obvious to everyone? How could you call on the French people to stand by "*la parole donnée*"[67] when you knew in your heart of hearts that the French people never gave it despite your efforts to compromise them and, moreover, that the Germans never stood by their part of the bargain. Did you not understand the complete absurdity of asking Frenchmen to continue respecting the forces who had been pillaging them for so long and whom even the man and woman in the street had learnt to despise. Indeed, instead of asking them to work with an invader whom they hated, you might usefully have released those who had taken an oath of fidelity to you. For if the Armistice still hung round your neck like a cannonball, it had long ceased to bind Frenchmen.

Now that the long-awaited "*jour de gloire est arrivé*"[68] once more, does not your warrior's heart vibrate to the sound of the Marseillaise echoing across the plains and mountains of France as Allied Armies sweep victoriously from West to East, and from South to North with, in the vanguard, the veteran divisions of Leclerc and de Lattre de Tassigny. Yes, your proud heart must accept reality. The other man, who foretold, at the darkest hour, France's triumph and proclaimed that a battle lost did not mean that the war was ended, has been proven right. Now you must admit that Frenchmen followed General de Gaulle in spirit and not yourself, and moreover, that their instinct was wholly justified.

Have you no qualms, Marshal Pétain, at having sent to their death, needlessly as it turns out, hundreds of brave men desirous of serving – humble, faithful souls whom you misled? Have you no regrets at having left Office – or rather that Office has left you – without your ever having publicly raised hand to *képi* in front of the mutilated bodies of the hostages assassinated by the Germans, as you did for the civilians bombed by the Allies? Were not the victims all equally subjects of the *Ėtat Français*? Regrets, remorse; these will be your punishments most surely, for no one can deny that your intentions were good. At the end of a glorious career you have failed in a great mission. Could there be anything more humiliating for the proudest, and the last, of

67. Word of honour.
68. Taken from the Marseillaise.

the Marshals of 1914–18? Yes, perhaps there could be, as when the SS squad came to drag you out of your bed at Vichy and conduct you to Germany. You had refused to leave France when expatriation, and a decision to continue the fight from North Africa, might have been a supreme service to *la Patrie*. You had sworn to remain in France, with the French people, through thick and thin, and your most earnest desire, now that Laval and his crew had fled, was, it seems, to be left in peace – such peace as your conscience gives you – *dans la France de vos amours* amidst the good people you tried to serve and ready to submit, if needs be, to whatever fate they might reserve for you. Even that humble desire was not to be and thus the proudest and the last of the glorious Marshals of 1914–18 crossed the frontier, a mere chattel, just another bit of loot in the baggage of the fleeing Hun.

An *adieu* you dictated while your gaolers were waiting at your bedroom door is being circulated hand-to-hand by faithful Frenchmen. To such an expedient for communicating your farewell message have your relations with the "honourable" adversary reduced you. Appended to the message is a text of your last missive to Hitler, bearing the same date (20 August 1944) and in which you reproached the Germans for having made misrepresentations to you. So at last you learnt your lesson. Too late, alas!

There is one consolation if your pride will allow you to accept pity. The good people of France do not wish you ill. Although they could not follow you, many are grateful for your presence in their midst during such sad and humiliating days, to some extent a willing scapegoat. Now that the French have recovered without you, and despite your misguided leadership, you may rest assured they bear you no grudge individually. They recognise the excellence of your intentions and feel nothing but pity for an unhappy old man. A Court may condemn you but they will absolve you. Many will still revere you, for you did your best. But your task was impossible. Taking honour as your guide and honesty as your weapon, you set out to contend with the Germans. You were Quixotic, they were Nazi. That explains everything.[69]

69. This chapter was finished in Biarritz at the end of 1944 after the Author had returned from Mont (70 kms inland), where he'd been exiled.

Chapter 15

Pierre Laval, the French Quisling

Pierre Laval cut a sorry figure in recent French history and, if ever, as has been said, appearance bears the clear imprint of fortune, this unprepossessing, dark, small *Auvergnat* carried his destiny for all to see – the ugly destiny of being branded an arch-traitor in a Nation of Patriots.

Until 1940 Pierre Laval's political career had been banal enough. He had shown himself to be clever, hard-working, ambitious; capable of insinuating himself with the best and the worst through the maze of political intrigue that became the norm for the Third Republic in its decline. He had filled high offices and earned the right to be addressed as *Monsieur le Président*, that hallmark of officialdom which leads sometimes to the Elysée. He had amassed considerable wealth but perhaps that did not count so much with him as ambition, for he longed to be a Mazarin or a Richelieu. Stubborn like all sons of Auvergne, he kept his counsel and knew his mind – a realist as well as a prince in an unscrupulous school. Perhaps he was nearest to a resounding success when he negotiated with Sir Samuel Hoare the still-born Hoare-Laval Pact, one of the pitiable might-have-beens of modern European history.

Here he is, emerging from the climactic cabinet meeting at Bordeaux, cool when many were flustered and deadly intent in his purpose of "saving France" by associating with her conqueror. There is no need to attribute to Pierre Laval any second thoughts on this occasion, when all Frenchmen were distraught by the catastrophe that had befallen their country. For a man patriotically-minded in his own way and who felt himself able enough, here was the double opportunity of satisfying ambition as well as serving his country according to his own way of thinking. His first problem was *Monsieur le Maréchal*, the outstanding personality which Fate had thrown up, a character both stubborn and proud. He quickly perceived that Marshal Pétain's prestige with the mass of Frenchmen could be made to yield the wherewithal to gild the bitter pill of the Armistice and he set himself the task of utilising the Marshal as his auxiliary, if not his tool. When the legendary defender of Verdun judged further resistance useless, who was to say nay? Thus the defeatists, led by Laval, gathered behind the old soldier, bowed with grief but imbued with the extravagant belief that he was the man of destiny sent to comfort France in her dire predicament.

Marshal Pétain surrendered to the Germans but the French Parliament surrendered to Pétain. Here was more of Laval's work. To secure this momentous constitutional change, it was necessary to persuade Parliament to relinquish its powers and President Lebrun his Seals of Office. Laval also needed to hold office himself in order to execute these major reforms. In the first Cabinet formed by the Marshal, when he took over from Paul Reynaud on 16 June, Laval's name did not figure. But once Mandel, Reynaud and Daladier had left, he appeared, first merely as *Ministre d'État,* but soon afterwards as Vice-Premier, a post shared for a few days with Camille Chautemps, until the latter, as if withered by Laval's presence, faded away. Laval was then free to take upon his shoulders and carry through, with a mastery all his own, the momentous task of transforming the political structure of France.

Untiringly, at Bordeaux, Clermont Ferrand and Vichy, he preached the necessity for the immediate modification not only of the constitution but also of the régime. In their daily meetings, the deputies and senators found him always at hand appealing, explaining, persuading; the hour was for action; there must be an end to discussions and debates. There would be no necessity to add a *coup d'état* to the misfortunes of France if only Deputies and Senators would prove reasonable. A régime responsible for war and defeat was obviously not qualified to negotiate peace. It was a sacred duty to ensure the continuity of France. Parliament alone could supply the means, according to Laval. His reasonings seemed to clinch it. Finally, on 4 July, in "the provisional Capital of

Free France", to give Vichy its pristine title, he put the problem in a nutshell by telling the Deputies that all Marshal Pétain required was a vote of confidence. The phrase had a familiar ring – Deputies and Senators had given many such. On such a momentous occasion, a large majority, or even, if possible, unanimity, was desirable. For this, Laval was helped by two Deputies; "the crucifixion of Parliament has become necessary", proclaimed Spinasse, a Socialist and former Minister under Léon Blum, "in order to prevent the nation sinking into violence and anarchy until the Government may be given the means of making a revolution without bloodshed. Let us seek a source of National Pride; all will be useless if we do not redeem our moral and spiritual weakness". This was strange language indeed, coming, as it did, from the mouth of a member of the fateful *Front Populaire.*[70]

Xavire Vallat, a member of the Right, was brief and incisive: "our institutions corrupted our men, now the institutions must be changed. But the men have also corrupted the institutions. It is therefore necessary to change the men so that France may live". Change the men! However, he proposed to deliver France over to the old stager Laval, notoriously one of the least respected of the Third Republic's politicians.

The Senators proved more troublesome to convince, but in the end both Houses fell into line. The Chamber of Deputies passed the motion to revise the constitution by 395 votes to 3 and the Senate did likewise by 229 to 1.

To complete the burying of the Constitution, a vote of both Houses, united in National Assembly, was necessary. It took place at Vichy on 10 July 1940. After a somewhat stormy debate the change was approved. The official record of the debate remained classified but was deposited in the National Archives for future reference.

A summary outlining the future Constitution and setting out which full powers were to be sought, was presented. It stated that lost battles must be turned to account, France remade. Regrets regarding the

70. Alliance of the Left in 1936 under Blum which brought about new social measures including the fortnight's paid holiday, the *congé payé*. Also accused of laxity and blamed for lack of military preparations.

extent of the defeat were useless. Other countries had found strength to reform despite internal disorder and defeat. Likewise France, at the cruellest moment in her history, must accept the necessity for a national revolution as the means of salvation. Frenchmen must bring to the new régime not just a resigned consent but an ardent faith, a complete gift of self, a supreme collective effort. Parliament would be honoured in history and deserve the gratitude of the nation for giving the example and opening wide the gates to the future. The Government must have full powers to save what might be saved, destroy what must be destroyed, build what must be built. The Assembly was therefore invited to place its confidence in Marshal Pétain to promulgate fundamental laws for the French State.

Defeatist doctrines thus glibly glossed over and disguised, there followed a project for a moderate corporative régime to function merely as the political organ for the assembly and unification of all the social forces and groups – family, professions, communes and regions, with the legitimate activities of each group to be subordinate to the general interest. The economy was to be reorganised, principally on an agricultural basis, with France becoming part of a continental system of production and exchange. There would be a new social order in which employers and employees would enjoy specific rights on the basis of collaboration under State control. Intelligence was to be the sole basis for advancement, and only one merit would be recognised, namely work, which would lead France to new destinies.

This project was Laval's masterpiece. Compared to other totalitarian Constitutions, it was moderate and reasonable and appeared to be inspired more by Salazar's model than Hitler's. It certainly wasn't possible to describe it in terms of wanting to imitate the Nazi régime.

The draft resolution, duly submitted to the Assembly, proposed to delegate to Marshal Pétain's Government full powers to promulgate by law a new French Constitution which would guarantee the rights of labour, of the family, and of the Nation. The Constitution was to be ratified by Assemblies created for such purpose.

The members of the Assembly, however, would not agree. A counter-draft was presented, whereby the Marshal was authorised to prepare but not to promulgate a new Constitution. Moreover, the Nation itself, not just the Assembly created by the Constitution, should be called upon to ratify it. Deputy Taurines, in presenting the counter-draft, recalled Marshal Pétain's declaration that he had no desire to be either a dictator or a Caesar. Finally, a compromise was reached proposing that the Constitution be ratified by the Nation and applied by the Assemblies to be created.

In the course of his persuasive speeches, Laval, as Marshal Pétain's mouthpiece, said that the Government had no intention of declaring war on England but, whenever possible, would hit back when hit. The extent of his prejudice against Great Britain may be measured when he said: "England dragged us into war but did nothing to help us to victory", and the degree of his misconception of the grand issue at stake in the world struggle can be understood from his declaration that "the greatest crime committed in our country is certainly to have declared war on Germany" but since France had gone to war and lost, the only thing to be done was to accept defeat and pay for it.

When, at last, the two Houses, united in National Assembly, voted the powers agreed upon as above, it was found that the opposition to the project which, in the separate votes of the Chamber of Deputies and Senate, had been only three and one vote respectively, had now risen to 80. Nevertheless, the new *Ėtat Français* came into existence on the handsome majority of 569 votes in a total House of 649 members. To secure the active majority required by the Constitution only 325 were needed. What a contrast to the abolished Constitution which, some sixty years earlier, had secured a majority of only one vote.

In justice, it would seem that blame must be attributed to the representatives of the French people for their action in committing hara-kiri at Laval's bidding. Dispirited at the mess into which they had got their country, they were only too ready to shirk their responsibilities and shift the burden. To all appearances, Fate, in finding a place such as the Casino at Vichy to house a surrender-minded Assembly, had perpetrated a last ghastly joke on Marianne.

The most that can be said of the proceedings is that they provided, in the opinion of eminent counsel, an irreproachable legal foundation for Marshal Pétain's régime, and that, in achieving this, Pierre Laval had brilliantly worked his ticket. An immediate reward came three days later when, by Constitutional Act No. 4, Marshal Pétain appointed him his successor-designate.

Laval swung rapidly into action. Abetz, the former spy, triumphantly back in Paris as German Ambassador, became Laval's closest associate and abettor. They arranged the infamous meeting between the ex-Corporal and the Marshal, which took place at Montoire, in the heart of the beautiful Vendomois country, and at which the policy of collaboration between the two countries was agreed. The photograph of the two leaders shaking hands immortalised the event. It was an unqualified success from Laval's point of view. Elated by the completeness and ease with which Pétain had appeared to accept the policy of collaboration, Laval proceeded to negotiate at a pace that outstripped all prudence. Knowing that other members of the Vichy Cabinet were, at heart, opposed to collaboration, Laval kept the negotiations to himself, so that, quite quickly, the Marshal gained the impression he was being outmanoeuvred and might, at any moment, be saddled with the *fait accompli* of an agreement between Laval and the Germans which it would be awkward, if not dangerous, for him to disavow.

Laval was probably intent on bouncing the elderly Marshal out of his determination to sit on the fence, however uncomfortably, until the war was over. For the Marshal, the Armistice was the code by which France was to be governed until the peace; for Laval, it was merely the first step towards a change of alliances to be effected with minimum delay.

Obviously someone was riding for a fall. It was Laval who came the cropper. His reticence backfired on him and proved his undoing. Time and again the Marshal had asked for a written report as to how negotiations with the Germans were going but, as so often, Laval put him off with one excuse or other.

The break came on the occasion of the Duc de Reichstadt celebrations, as the Germans called them, or the Roi de Rome funeral, as the French regarded the matter, arranged to take place in Paris in December 1940. Everything had been prepared for an elaborate ceremony in a grandiose setting, a theatrical historic scene dear to the teutonic heart, that was to seal reconciliation between the French and German peoples. The presence in Paris of Marshal Pétain and Hitler was designed to complete the picture. Abetz was so sure of his guests that a special menu for the dinner at the German Embassy was prepared. However, there is many a slip twixt cup and lip. At the last hour the Marshal became suspicious and refused to budge. Hitler had to remain in Germany. Admiral Darlan's blue and gold, though decorative, proved a poor substitute for the Marshal's stars. However, the Admiral carried in his pocket his letter of appointment as Dauphin.

The news that Laval had been disgraced spread like wildfire in France. It caused perhaps even more of a stir in Germany. However, there it was; the old Marshal was to some extent still master in his own house. Hitler invited the Admiral to Berchtesgaden and gave him a thorough dressing-down.

As a result, the men who had laid obstacles in Laval's path at Vichy, namely Baudoin, Alibert, Peyrouton and Flandin, were removed and the Marshal consented to meeting Laval again and offering him a seat in Government once more. Laval refused. This may well have displeased the Germans but he was on his dignity and they could not force their horse to drink. However, they continued to back him steadily while he, operating in an underworld of intrigue, showed himself a willing tool in a ghastly conspiracy to exploit France to the full. Many months were then to elapse before Laval at last obtained full control in November 1942 when von Runstedt overran the Vichy Zone in response to the Allies' invasion of North Africa.

Darlan's defection at Algiers was a hard blow for the Marshal personally but a trump card for Laval, whose influence over affairs at

Vichy from that moment went from strength to strength. He was able to harness Henriot's shoddy eloquence to the propaganda chariot and set Darnand's militia to track down the patriots. However, try as he might, Laval could not make Frenchmen take Henriot seriously nor furnish the 200,000 recruits Darnand was calling for. All he could do was rope in those fanatics whose fear of bolshevism (the greater number) and distrust of "perfidious Albion" (the few) overrode all else, and thus maintain a semblance of hitching France to the German chariot.

Initially, during the years of German triumph, while Hitler pulled off success after success and the German Army marched from Berlin to the four winds of the compass in Europe, the North Cape, Finistère, Salonika and Stalingrad, for one who both believed in and desired Germany's victory, Pierre Laval's conduct was logical and his actions were inasmuch justified. For many years, he had foreseen the danger for the nation in crossing Germany's path and had disapproved of the alliances made by France, which rendered a clash inevitable. France's position in Europe and the world was such that she could make her presence felt. If this was not enough, she possessed sufficient resources and abundance of territories in her vast Empire to drive useful bargains. By 1940, although the privileged pre-war position she enjoyed had been seriously curtailed by military defeat, there still remained enough to exploit if, by a rapid volte face, the new French régime put itself on the winning side, or at least one which at the time seemed incontestably the winning side.

Laval might have succeeded but for the hitch in December 1940. Before he could decently worm his was back into office at Vichy, the opportunity had passed, French National opinion had hardened and the Marshal may have sensed it, for he had to be driven from position to position before apparently succumbing.

After the Armistice there was undoubtedly scope for a policy of working with Germany as well as rebuilding France on new lines of corporativism. There seemed to be a legitimate field for collaboration, which accounts for the initial favour that policy met with in considerable circles of French life. But later, when the general repugnance of the

Nation for it was more evident, while moreover Germany's failure to merge domination in Europe with meaningful development became obvious, as well as her declining military power, upon which all else depended, then Laval's efforts became eminently treasonable and the thousands of workers he sent to Germany were so many hostages delivered blindly, if not in cold blood, to a cruel fate. For Laval was too intelligent not to be able to read the writing on the wall.

Where Laval differed from the Marshal as a collaborationist was that he accepted German hegemony from the first and concentrated on bringing France into line, in the hope no doubt of making her the pre-eminent satellite in the grand new constellation subordinating France's reconstruction to incorporation in the German system; whereas the Marshal, with greater native prudence, was more intent on laying new foundations, especially in the moral field, which in all events would serve a useful purpose.

The Marshal might claim to remain *l'homme de la France* but Laval became that ignominious figure, *l'homme de l'Allemagne.*

Chapter 16

The Hour of Truth: 6 June 1944

One mighty blow and a considerable stretch of the famous and formidable wall against invasion from the North and West is smashed, British tenacity vindicated, and St. Nazaire April 1942 and Dieppe August 1942 avenged. The French proverb *jamais deux sans trois,* printed by the Germans across photographs of those tragic events, is given the lie. The breaching of the terrible obstacle so diligently constructed over a period of four years, and proclaimed impregnable, spells dire defeat for German power and prestige. 'Collaboration', based on intimidation, receives a knock-out blow.

It also means, however, that the full destructive power of the Anglo-American Air Force falls on Normandy and the valleys of the Seine and the Loire – a tornado engulfing in death and ruin thousands of innocent people, as well as broad acres of fertile countryside. Yet another frightful ordeal for France, already on the rack. What counts most, however, even in the minds of most of the victims, is the resultant German discomfort. A ready yardstick to measure this is provided by one of the numerous pamphlets provided by the Germans in their efforts to rouse French opinion. "The Atlantic Fortress – from Vauban to Todt", sold in French bookstalls and railway stations for ten francs. The publication is a typical production of German propaganda, a mixture of cunning and stupidity, albeit having some technical merit. Numerous illustrations, reproductions of ancient engravings and plans, plus modern photographs extending over a wide range of material, all show that Teutonic noses have poked into the remotest corners of French libraries, national, provincial and private, during the years of occupation.

"*Les forteresses de l'Atlantique contre l'Angleterre 1943*" (as per the subtitle) purports to be the first of a series of pamphlets destined to show how it is that the German Army comes to be substituted for the French in the defence of the seaboard. The compiler, one Dr. W.

Brepohl, explains that the German soldiers well understand the meaning of their watch over the French coast of the Atlantic and North Sea, keeping guard not only over Germany but over Europe as well. The task assumed by the true soldiers of Europe is not new. What is new is that it should be German soldiers, and not the French themselves, who mount that guard. Whereas over centuries the best Kings of France repulsed English encroachments, the Frenchmen of today no longer heed their historical duties but live under the spell of England's pretended friendship and so, unconsciously, lie to themselves. They fail to see the true vision of Perfidious Albion.

Dr. Brepohl further goes on to explain how the Führer, realising how necessary it was to be strong in defence against the English, set the German architect Todt on the path of the great Vauban to build, on modern lines, with cement and steel, a coastal rampart capable of withstanding the most violent assaults.

Dr. Brepohl refers to a number of historical events to support these themes of Perfidious Albion and valiant defence.

The ill-fated attempt by an Anglo-Dutch fleet in 1694 to put an expeditionary force ashore serves to stress, in an unconvincing way, a supposed analogy between the problems of 1694 and those of today. "Then, as now, the continent only knew one enemy. It was the great merit of Vauban to have strained every effort to oppose the eternal enemy. He foresaw where the invaders would land and was waiting for them." It is difficult to say that Todt has been right in this respect.

Stories of resistance to England's rising naval power and of attempts to break her Continental Blockade provide Hitler's propogandist with abundant material. Various trivialities are served up, mingled with reproductions of old charts and use of current-day photographs, in an effort to touch chords of anti-English feeling long since gone in the French mindset, put aside by the Entente Cordiale.

The Brepohl pamphlet also draws heavily on the Napoleonic epoch with its mooted plans for the invasion of England. Pictures of a channel tunnel and of fleets of *montgolfières* carrying infantry, cavalry and guns, and thoughts of what Fulton might have done to Nelson's fleet, fall flat in the face of Allied power and the absence of U-boats from the channel. Frenchmen listening to the thrilling reality of thousands of heavy bombers over Berlin smile at the unconvincing effort put together by the German propogandist. The book cover displays Vauban next to Todt with a ferocious French corsair, axe in hand, calling to his countrymen: "France is the advanced bastion of Europe, defend her", supported by a quotation from Guy de Maupassant "I hate the English". Such incongruities seem destined solely to achieve success for collectors of the picturesque. Yet they were as much part of the German effort as Hitler's ravings and Göring's boasts.

The last pages of the pamphlet reproduce a paragraph written by a French journalist after being taken on a conducted tour of the Western Wall. "I have witnessed scenes of desolation which beggar description. In case of disembarkation the rampart of the Atlantic protects us against danger and we know very well that it would keep the war far from our coasts. If the German Army watch over the war it is naturally in German interests that they do so, but it would also be in English and American interests to reflect thrice before attacking such a rampart. What interests me for my country is that France should be able to live on in peace and security, safe from future disruptions". Poor deluded soul.

Summing up, Dr Brepohl claims that "three factors saved France from invasion on former occasions – a passive element consisting of the particular nature of the coastline, an active element in the patriotism of local populations, and a decisive element, namely Vauban's magnificent fortifications. The first element remains. As to the second, many Frenchmen have become 'waiters' and imagine that the painful situation to which they have been reduced by irresponsible leaders will settle itself. They listen to the BBC, forgetting that the British remain the hereditary enemy and that they constitute the same danger for peace as always! We are obsessed by the desire to show them these photographs and to say: 'Look, thus should you take position in the new Europe, exactly as of yore Richelieu, Louis XIV and Napoleon acted. Vauban was Louis' Todt, whose ramparts, reinforced by us, stand against the same enemy today."

Tosh! The wall has been breached. A long section with the cornerstone of Cherbourg has collapsed under the power of weapons forged in England and America, and thanks to the valour of the men who wielded them. Prophets are confounded: the Italian Admiral Oscar de Giamberardino, who wrote in his treatise on the art of war at sea (1939), "naval actions against coastlines have only a demonstrative interest and do not justify the risks they entail", as well as the German General von der Boltz, who collectively condemned amphibian operations, have both been proven utterly wrong, as also have the numerous writers who affirmed that the success of operations, mainly depending on surprise, could not be ensured under modern conditions. "Almost certainly, air reconnaissance will discover departure preparations, allowing more or less accurate conjecture as regards disembarkation points. Thus, the defenders will be able to attack convoys and accumulate defence preparations at the threatened points".

None of this was to happen. Eisenhower, emulating William the Conqueror but in the other direction, made for the estuary of the Seine and managed to get there undetected. How this was achieved was one of the mysteries of the war because a fortnight before the landing, Berlin communiqués were mentioning convoy preparations in the Bristol Channel and on the southwest coast. The complete failure of the Luftwaffe and U-boats to take a punitive toll of the unprecedented mass of shipping concentrated for the operation is astounding. Such missed opportunities spelled disaster for German arms. The capture of Cherbourg exactly three weeks after the landings completed the debacle.

The disembarkation, tardy perhaps but happening at last, was hailed with joy by the French people, to whom it brought the beginnings of liberation from the intolerable burden of occupation and slavery. The French mind was quick to grasp, however, that the landing site, situated so far west, spelled ruin for the fairest lands of France. Feelings were necessarily mixed as apprehension rose regarding the price of liberation. It threatened to be crushing.

The battle for France would have to be fought, not as hoped, in Belgium, Holland or Germany, but in the heart of France. What a prospect, should, as seemed probable, German resistance prove as stubborn as in Russia; dire devastation, as in the Ukraine, sweeping from Normandy to the Rhine, engulfing Paris.

Official statistics of damage to property in France, up to 1 January 1944, showed that bombardment, since the Armistice, had already done far more damage than the military operations of 1939–40 and that, all-in-all, approximately as many French houses had been destroyed as during 1914–18. Since the beginning of the year, however, when British and American bombers had begun preparing for invasion, the toll on life and property had been increasing dramatically. Rouen lay in ruins, like St. Nazaire and Lorient, and there was hardly a French town of any size from Le Havre to Marseille, from Brest to Epinal, which had not suffered. According to figures published before the landing, loss of life and property in France, due to British and American bombs, was already comparable to the damage done by the Germans to England. Such widespread destruction, with its sacrifice of innocent civilians, constituted a terrible reflection on modern methods of warfare. The letter of the French Cardinals to their British and American brethren embodied a piteous and impotent protest. The onslaught would have to continue.

Vae Victis, the woe called down on the vanquished in 1940, could not be easily appeased. Not satisfied with four years of sequestration of the manhood of the nation, privation for the women folk, under-nourishment for the children, impoverishment and slavery for the rest, there had to be blood. Blood that France could least afford. It was furthermore decreed that political rivalries and hatred amongst Frenchmen would be let loose; the hideous dragon of disorder raise its head. To the hostages shot by the Germans in cold blood, the riddled bodies hanging on the bridge at Avignon, on the Square at Pau and in many other French towns, had to be added the toll of the assassinated, Frenchmen of one class or opinion by Frenchmen of another, and all the others, old and young, pêle-mêle crushed under falling masonry or directly by the bombs of their liberators. What a tragedy! Small wonder some flinched and would have bought peace at any price. The greater wonder was that, despite German and Vichy propaganda, despite the natural weakness of the flesh, there would be such general comprehension and acceptance of sacrifice among non-combatants who were destined to be the victims of the fight for liberation. There was no flight from Paris this time. Everyone remained awaiting the return to normal life. Oh if that could only be a prelude to a wider return to sanity on the part of the Nations of the world!

Appendix
The Spanish Refugees

In the tragedy of France, other men, women and children suffered, along with the French. At the crossroads of Europe, France, for centuries, had been the traditional haven for refugees of diverse backgrounds. Some were desirable citizens, others less so; not a few were criminals, clinging to a political excuse. All were caught in the net of the Armistice, with the exception of those able to procure passage on refugee ships or save themselves by gain of their money or at the cost of hazardous adventure.

Those most in peril were the unfortunate Germans and Italians who had fled from the embrace of Hitler and Mussolini, together with Austrians, Czechs, Poles, Russians and Jews, victims of one of the most terrible persecutions in history.

In a category apart, sharing in every way the privations of the French, and with many anxieties of their own, were the remnants of the 400,000 republican, socialist, anarchist, syndicalist and communist Spaniards who had fled before the avenging sword of General Franco early in 1939. For days the torrent had poured into Cerdagne by Hannibal's ancient pass, or had crowded the international tunnel, finally to throng the miserable improvised camps on the mistral-swept beaches at Argelès.[71] For weeks, families and their flocks, plus innumerable ragged stragglers, covered every track leading to the rugged Cerbères Hills and braved the icy slopes of Canigou. There was many an obscure tragedy when some exhausted, pneumonia-stricken human fell by the way dotted with foundered dead or dying beasts of burden. The congestion in the camps claimed more victims. But, in an astonishingly short time, considering their numbers, their destitution and the difficulties in their path, most

71. Town in south-east France, on the Mediterranean.

of the refugees found their way out of the camps and dispersed all over France. Leading communists, including the dour, crime-laden peasant, El Campesino, the young sectarian, Jesus Hernandez, and the fiery Pasionaria, found haven in Russia, whence to continue, at a safe distance, the campaign against Franco's fascism. Several years later, the hectic tones of Hernandez's oratory and the impassioned accent of the "Passion Flower" (a heavy, sharp-featured matron) were still coming over the wireless from the land of the Soviets, unchastened by alliance with Hitler and the disastrous result of the "Eternal Peace" then sworn. The international schemers who had descended to prey upon Spain during the revolution, many of them unable to return home, sought protection in diverse sectors of French politics. The Commission, led by a British General, engaged in the repatriation of the rank and file of the International Brigades – as consented by the Republican Government in a last, though useless, sacrifice on the altar of Non-Intervention – did manage to save a few shiploads of emigrants. Many refugee Republican Ministers followed the gold of Spain to Mexico and used some of it to charter ships for their marooned followers. Several Central American Republics offered facilities.

A great number of those who fled, especially the Catalan villagers, had taken to their heels quite unnecessarily. Forerunners of the millions of Belgians and French who were to be seized by the self-same panic, these poor folk realised their mistake and mostly returned to Spain when the Civil War ended. The greater bulk of the refugees, with the astonishing faculty of adaptation that has made Spain one of the pioneering nations, managed to fend for themselves, seeking pastures new as far afield as the Philippines. Many thousands remained in hospitable France, dispersed like rain and, like it, absorbed into the soil. Engaged in many menial capacities, exercising a hundred humble crafts, living in dignified poverty or at relative ease, they settled down to await events in Spain, imbued with fatalism. "He who waiteth long enough will see the corpse of his enemy carried by".

The Spanish War had been cleverly used by Germany, Italy and Russia to further not only their political aims but as a testing ground for their military equipment and theories. Over Spanish towns and fields, squadrons of bomber and fighter planes clashed. Franco's victory was to a great extent a triumph of Axis armament. Thus, when some six months after the momentous exodus across the Pyrenees, the Second World War began in earnest, the exiled President Don Manuel Azaña, may well have exclaimed: "The war begun in Spain will end there". Mobilisation in France brought many unsought opportunities of employment for the Spanish refugees. In a hundred walks of life in office and factory they stepped into the shoes of the conscripted, helped by their native adaptability and gift for picking up languages. A number enlisted in the French Army, while from the able-bodied in the camps a Labour Corps was constituted which helped to cover the northern frontier with trenches and redoubts which were to prove supremely useless, though by no fault of the diggers.

Whilst there were undoubted employment opportunities, France's collapse proved a calamity for the refugees. All foreigners became suspect for the new *Ėtat Français*, in particular former stalwarts of the *Frente Popular.* Thus, Spanish men found themselves once again rounded up in concentration camps, in particular the spacious enclosure at Gurs, which the unfortunate Basques had at one time planned to turn into a "Guernica Reborn". There, in the huts on the banks of the Gave d'Oloron,[72] in view of the glorious mountains, many a poor Spaniard found himself again at the parting of the ways. Worse still, General Franco, once baulked of his prey, had not relinquished revenge. He claimed and secured from the Gestapo in occupied France a number of prominent refugees whom he promptly shot. Among these unfortunates were Lluis Companys, President of the Catalan Generalitat, and the Basque Juan Zugazagoita, a former Minister of the Interior. With greater luck, José Antonio Aguirre, President of the short-lived Basque Republic, slipped through the net and managed to reach Scandinavia. Lister, a quarryman from Galicia, who rose to the rank of Corps Commander in the Republican Army, travelled

72. A *gave* is a Pyrenean river near its starting point. Oloron a small town not far from the Pyrenees, about 60 kms from the Atlantic.

to England and, it was reported, secured a commission in the Allied Forces before meeting a soldier's death in the Abyssinian campaign. Airmen, dispersed to the four winds by the Republican defeat, later found occasion to fight once more in a bigger and worthier cause. Marshall Tito's experiences in the International Brigade served him in good stead as leader of the Yugoslav patriots.

As many Spaniards as could manage it remained near the frontier. There the Germans found them, sometimes holding conversations across the Bidasoa with relatives in Spain. Many a parent caught his first sight of offspring as babes or little children were held up among the maize fields fringing the narrow waters. The more favoured secured real meetings at the French end of the International bridge at Hendaye where, on a bench placed by kindly *douaniers*,[73] families sat and talked. The Germans removed the bench and painted a line across the road, some yards from the bridge, indicating the limit beyond which no one might pass without special authority. There one might occasionally see a mother leading little children to be transferred to the care of grandparents in Spain for the better food across the border. One day, two elderly people appeared at the Spanish end of the bridge and walked across to where the German sentry at the French end halted them. Expostulation from the voluble Spaniards pointing towards a mother and two small children. It was the children who broke the deadlock by scampering across the intervening space and taking refuge in Grandma's voluminous skirts. The kissing and hugging which ensued produced a wave of emotion that overcame even the sentry, who permitted the old lady to step across and then embrace the weeping, already lonely, mother, whilst the children remained in Grandpa's care until Grannie returned, when the pair departed, leading two new little citizens back to Spain.

Not all was innocence and candour on the frontier. What glances of fear and hate as well as of love and yearning have been cast across those dividing waters where thousands crossed their Rubicon, hard

73. Customs officers.

by the muddy islet once painted by Velazquez as a meeting place for Kings. The frontier, for years a noted centre of international intrigue, remained so despite the strict supervision by the Germans. They dealt a shrewd blow, however, when they expelled *en masse* to Vichy the crowd of petty diplomatic representatives from almost every country in the world which had gathered in the land of the Basques.

When war broke out in 1939 the sympathies of the refugees were all with France. Nevertheless, within a year, force of circumstance gathered many of them into the German net. Once the Armistice signed, Hitler's agents were quick to realise the opportunity before them. The refugees were a source of anxiety as well as a problem of cost to the French Government and thus, when the Germans asked to be allowed to recruit workers in the camps, there was no objection. The refugees themselves jumped at the offer to exchange the semi-starvation and irksome constraint of the camps for fields of new adventure. The Germans fed and paid them well, with extra allowances for work in bombed areas. Occasional short periods of leave were granted with permission to travel in occupied France. Spaniards built the submarine bases at La Rochelle and Lorient; they worked at Nantes, Brest and Dunkirk, and even in the Channel Islands.

German cunning found the means to empty some of Franco's prisons as well as the French camps. Numbers of Basque separatists belonging to seafaring pursuits thus got an unlooked-for opportunity, readily seized, to exchange imprisonment in Bilbao for well-paid services on ships employed in the coastal trade for the Germans. They brought news from Spain to the refugees in France and conveyed messages back from them. Needless to say, the refugees, irrespective of masters, remained a fraternity.

All-in-all, they served the Germans well on sea and land from Bayonne to Hamburg although – by an irony of fate – all the hard work they put in on the Rampart of the Atlantic proved as useless as the fortifications dug in 1939 for the Allies. Nonetheless, the events at St. Nazaire, where Spanish workers sided and suffered with

French civilians who helped the Kommando troops, showed that their sympathies remained steadfastly with the Allies.

Their great chance came with the *Maquis* movement. Here was a sort of warfare the ex-militiamen understood. They deserted the Germans and joined up in their thousands. Among the guerrilla bands in Savoie, the Massif Central, Brittany and the Pyrenees, Spanish fighters distinguished themselves in ambushing small parties of Germans, waylaying convoys and blowing up railway tracks and bridges. It was curious to find that when the Germans executed Alfonso, one of the *Maquis* leaders in Savoie, even the Phalangist press in Spain took pride in pointing out his fortitude and bravery. It may truly be said that the part played by Spanish volunteers in helping to liberate France was a considerable one. Later, when arms came to hand and the guerrilleros merged into the army of the *Maquis,* some 15,000 Spaniards, organised in Corps Francs under their own officers, took part in hounding the Germans from the Pyrenees and the plains of Languedoc and Guyenne. These Spaniards hoped that, in return for their part in liberating France, French comrades would help them liberate Spain from fascism. They burned to renew against Franco the struggle for the Republic. Their numbers, the cohesion they had established and the sympathies they had gained, not to speak of the arms they now possessed, made them a considerable factor in the changing world at Toulouse. They disposed of a wireless station, Radio España Independiente, broadcasting four times a day on shortwave, as well as several newspapers, of which two were in Castillian: *La Reconquista de España,* organ of the *Union Nacional,* the Spanish Republican party, and *La Lucha*, a communist paper. *Foc Nou*, a Catalan separatist organ, appeared in Catalan.

Enthusiasm ran high among the refugees. At Montauban, a mass meeting was held over the tomb of Don Manuel Azaña, the late President of the Spanish Republic, whose above-mentioned prophecy that the World War begun in Spain would end there, was yet perhaps to come true. At Pau and elsewhere, bands of overzealous Spanish *Maquisards* kidnapped Franco's Consular Representatives but the bewildered officials were rescued before the incidents could attain international importance. Long vigil in exile was making Spanish refugees desperate. Their continued presence in France confronted the new French Government with an urgent problem.

Five years on from the end of the Civil War no general political amnesty had yet been granted. A great opportunity had been lost by the new Spanish régime to recover a valuable element of the human capital of the country. Meanwhile, butchers, bakers and candlestick makers, farmers, fishermen and doctors, shoe-blacks, shop-keepers and proctors, professors, musicians and magistrates, painters, poets and sculptors, priests, bishops, and even a cardinal, all awaited the opportunity of returning. In Biarritz, amidst choir books and choristers, gentle Padre Donostia continued discoursing sweet music. The Cardinal-Archbishop of Tarragona prayed in Rome. Professor Altamira, Judge on the Tribunal at the Hague and an eminent historian, wrote industriously at Bayonne, as did Señor Perez de Ayala, the novelist-diplomat, in South America.

In one respect, the Spaniards were irrepressible: they continued to marry and multiply, for that is the first law of Spanish stock wherever it be, the secret of vigorous survival through centuries of disaster.